JOSEPH HOROWITZ is Manager, Planning and Design, Facilities Engineering Department, Columbia Broadcasting System, Inc., and a Consultant in critical path scheduling. In the latter capacity he has developed and conducted successful training programs for a number of professional groups. During a tour of duty with the United States Navy Civil Engineer Corps, he was in charge of planning and design of training and other military facilities in the United States and Japan. Later he served as Chief Engineer for Tumpane Co., Inc., supervising design, construction, and facilities planning for the United States Air Force in Ankara, Turkey. Mr. Horowitz is a member of the American Society of Civil Engineers, the National Society of Professional Engineers, and the American Association of Cost Engineers.

Critical Path Scheduling

MANAGEMENT CONTROL
THROUGH *CPM* AND *PERT*

JOSEPH HOROWITZ

COLUMBIA BROADCASTING SYSTEM, INC.

ROBERT E. KRIEGER PUBLISHING COMPANY
MALABAR, FLORIDA

Original Edition 1967
Reprint Edition 1980 with corrections

Printed and Published by
ROBERT E. KRIEGER PUBLISHING COMPANY, INC.
KRIEGER DRIVE
MALABAR, FLORIDA 32950

Copyright © 1967 by
THE RONALD PRESS COMPANY
Reprinted by Arrangement with
JOHN WILEY & SONS, INC.

Printed in the United States of America

Library of Congress Cataloging in Publication Data

Horowitz, Joseph.
    Critical path scheduling.

    Reprint of the ed. published by Ronald Press Co.,
New York.
    Bibliography: p.
    Includes index.
    1. Critical path analysis. I. Title.
[TS158.H63 1980]   658.4'032   79-25305
ISBN 0-89874-089-4

10 9 8 7 6 5 4

Preface

The Critical Path Method (CPM) is a powerful new management tool that is gaining increasing acceptance in industry and business. In the few years since its inception, hundreds of articles, papers, and books have been published on the subject. However, in the search for a clear and complete description of the techniques, the author found most of the published materials to be either too elementary, offering only the basic mechanics of CPM with little attention to applications, or too specialized, emphasizing the underlying mathematical theory.

This book has been designed to provide an understandable but comprehensive introduction to CPM and its companion network method, PERT (Program Evaluation and Review Technique), and their applications. Basic principles are presented in simple language with numerous illustrations and examples. For the most part, the methods used require only elementary arithmetic or simple graphs. No knowledge of advanced mathematics is assumed or required. The book is intended to be useful to business and industrial managers as well as to architects and engineers.

It is the author's conviction that CPM is primarily a *method* or discipline of planning, rather than a computer application, although it can make good use of computers. For this reason, manual (non-computer) methods have been emphasized throughout the book. It should also be pointed out that manual methods have certain advantages over machine methods in some applications. Computers have not been ignored, however, and two chapters are devoted to computer applications and the selection of a computer program. Another chapter is concerned with the problems of introducing CPM into a company and the setting up of administrative procedures necessary to make it work in organizations of various types.

The text is accompanied by problems, and solutions are provided at the end of the book. This gives the reader needed practice in testing his knowledge as he goes along, with the opportunity to check his results.

The author wishes to express his appreciation to Michael N. Salgo, P.E., Director, Facilities Engineering, Columbia Broadcasting System, for his stimulation and encouragement in this field; to Isaac W. Tarshansky, P.E., for his review of the manuscript and valuable suggestions; to Henry Granet for painstaking preparation of the diagrams; and, finally, to his wife, Carol, for her patience and forbearance.

JOSEPH HOROWITZ

New York, New York
January, 1967

Contents

Critical Path Scheduling

MANAGEMENT CONTROL
THROUGH *CPM* AND *PERT*

1

CPM and PERT–An Overview

WHAT IS CPM?

The Critical Path Method (CPM) is a system for *planning, scheduling,* and *controlling* a project. In CPM the steps or operations necessary to complete the project are shown in a graph called a *network*. The network also shows the order in which the operations must be completed: which tasks can be done together, and which must follow other operations.

When the network is complete, the planner estimates how long it will take to do each operation. Obviously, the time for completing the entire project is not the sum of the individual operation times, since some things can be done at the same time. Actually, a small number of operations control the project completion time. These tasks, called *critical operations,* form a chain through the network called the *critical path*. This is the origin of the name Critical Path Method.

Knowing the critical path is of great value in planning and controlling the project. Users have found that they can get meaningful answers to such questions as:

How long will the project take? Can we meet our contract completion date?

If there is a delay in one activity, will the entire project be delayed? If so, by how much?

What is the most economical way to speed up the project?

How can we tell whether we are on schedule while there is still time to take corrective action?

How can we schedule our manpower to avoid excessive ups and downs without delaying project completion?

How can we schedule material deliveries so as to have things on the job when needed but avoid costly storage for long periods?

WHEN CAN YOU USE CPM?

To be able to use CPM, the project must have a definite beginning and a definite end. It must also be made up of a series of smaller jobs or operations that must be done in an orderly sequence to complete the project. A good example is building a house: the foundations precede the wall, the shingles must follow the roof boards, etc. Construction projects of all types lend themselves to CPM scheduling, and the construction industry was among the first to make widespread use of the method. CPM is equally suitable for planning any one-time project such as:

1. Setting up a new department
2. Introducing a new product
3. Research and development projects
4. Engineering or architectural design
5. Producing a Broadway play or a television show
6. Assembling a large piece of machinery or aircraft

The method does not lend itself to flow-type work, such as an assembly line, although it would be useful for setting up a new assembly line.

CPM and related techniques have been widely accepted in government, the armed forces, and particularly in the aerospace industry, where designers and manufacturers have found them invaluable in controlling the complex sequence of operations involved in developing and producing rockets and weapons systems.

CPM AND PERT

CPM is one of a family of planning techniques, which includes PERT (Program Evaluation and Review Technique), among many others. These systems were developed and refined by many different companies and government agencies, with the result that there are various names in use for similar systems. In addition to CPM and PERT, there are CPS (Critical Path Scheduling), LESS (Least Cost Estimating and Scheduling), PEP (Program Evaluation Procedure), and others. All are really variations of the two basic systems: CPM and PERT. CPM and PERT have much in common. In this text CPM will be presented first, and PERT will be introduced as a variation of the basic CPM system.

HISTORY OF CPM AND PERT

The techniques of critical path scheduling were developed independently in two parallel, but slightly different, programs. In 1957 a team of engineers and mathematicians from Du Pont and the Sperry Rand Corporation developed a management control system that was used successfully for scheduling complicated design, construction, and plant maintenance projects. This system became known as the *Critical Path Method.*

At about the same time, the Navy was looking for a system to manage and control the Fleet Ballistic Missile Program, which produced the Polaris missile. Working with a firm of management consultants and with Lockheed, the prime contractor, the Navy Special Projects Office, in 1958, developed a management control system that was called PERT (Program Evaluation and Review Technique).

In the Polaris missile program the Navy was faced with the job of coordinating the work of some 3,000 contractors, suppliers, and government agencies involved in design, development, and fabrication. The coordination proved so effective that PERT was credited by the Navy with advancing the successful completion of the Polaris program by more than 2 years.

Although they originally differed in approach and philosophy, PERT and CPM have much in common. Both make use of the fundamental technique of showing the project by means of a diagram of arrows and circles called a *network* or *arrow diagram.* PERT has found increasing use in planning and control of military and aerospace projects and has been gradually spreading throughout industry generally. CPM has been most widely accepted by construction firms, who find it superior to older methods for scheduling and controlling the one-of-a-kind type of project typified by a construction job. The subsequent development of PERT and CPM—and a host of offshoots and similar systems—has greatly expanded their usefulness. At the same time, some of the distinctions that originally existed have tended to disappear.

Because both CPM and PERT made use of the capabilities of electronic data processing equipment (computers), manufacturers of this equipment have been active in developing the concepts and publicizing the methods. A number of consulting firms have also specialized in this field and have conducted courses and training programs to familiarize industry with these techniques. Today courses are offered by universities as well as by professional and management associations.

CPM is now a well-accepted technique in many fields, particularly construction. It is not uncommon for contract specifications to require its use on government projects or those connected with space technology.

A SAMPLE PROJECT—OFF TO WORK *

To see just what is meant by CPM, consider the simple "project" of getting the master of the house off to work in the morning. Assume that he is required to be at work at 8:30 A.M. The tasks or operations that must be performed each morning to accomplish this project are listed below (not necessarily in order) together with the time each operation takes. For what time should he set the alarm?

Operation	Time in Minutes
Rise, wake wife, start coffee	5
Coffee brews	10
Wife gets up, dresses, cooks breakfast	35
Shower	8
Drink first cup of coffee	5
Shave and dress	15
Eat breakfast and drink second cup of coffee	15
Drive to work	30

* The author is indebted to Mr. George W. Ullrich (formerly on active duty with the U. S. Navy Civil Engineer Corps) for the original version of this problem, which was developed by Mr. Ullrich for a CPM course given at the U. S. Navy Construction Battalion Center, Davisville, R.I.

Let us see what happens if we analyze this project. As soon as the alarm goes off, our hero gets up, wakes the assistant project manager (wife), and starts the coffee. Let us show this first operation by means of an arrow (Fig. 1–1).

RISE, WAKE WIFE, START COFFEE
5

Fig. 1–1

There is no particular scale to the arrow, but the estimated time (5 minutes) is shown immediately underneath it. The coffee now brews while the man showers. Both "coffee brews" and "shower" can start as soon as the first operation is finished, and both can proceed simultaneously, as shown in Fig. 1–2.

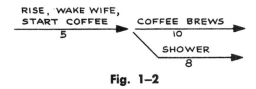

RISE, WAKE WIFE,
START COFFEE
5
COFFEE BREWS
10
SHOWER
8

Fig. 1–2

When both these operations are completed, the husband can drink the first cup of coffee. This is shown by another arrow, starting from the point where the two previous arrows ended (Fig. 1–3).

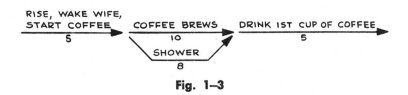

RISE, WAKE WIFE,
START COFFEE
5
COFFEE BREWS
10
SHOWER
8
DRINK 1ST CUP OF COFFEE
5

Fig. 1–3

While all of this is going on, the wife is getting up, dressing, and preparing breakfast. To show this, we draw another parallel arrow, starting from the end of the first operation (Fig. 1–4).

Fig. 1–4

Returning to the husband, "shave and dress" is next, followed by "eat breakfast and drink second cup of coffee." However, the eating cannot start unless breakfast is ready. This is shown in Fig. 1–5.

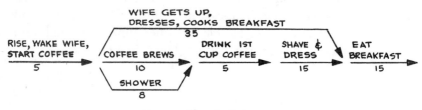

Fig. 1–5

Driving to work completes the project, as shown in Fig. 1–6.

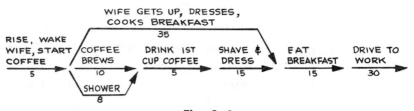

Fig. 1–6

To find out how long the entire project will take, all we have to do is add up the times along each chain of arrows through the diagram. The chain with the greatest total time gives us the time for the project. In this example the uppermost chain of arrows adds up to the longest time: 85 minutes. Since this equals 1 hour 25 minutes, the alarm should be set for 7:05 A.M.

The chain of tasks or operations that determines the overall job duration is shown by a heavy line in Fig. 1–7. If any of these operations takes longer than expected, the total project time will be increased accordingly.

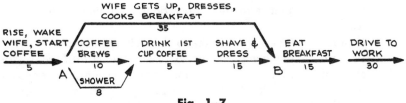

Fig. 1–7

On the other hand, consider the lower chain of arrows, between points A and B in Fig. 1–7. Choosing the longer of the two paths, these operations consume 30 minutes as follows:

Coffee brews	10
Drink first cup of coffee	5
Shave and dress	15
Total	30

Compare this total to the heavy arrow A–B in Fig. 1–7, which takes 35 minutes. This means that a delay of less than 5 minutes in the lower chain of operations will not affect the project time.

This example illustrates the essence of the Critical Path Method. The chain of operations that determines total project time is known as the *critical path*, and these operations are called *critical operations*. Similarly, the other operations are *noncritical;* they can be delayed to some extent without affecting the total project time.

The critical path determines the time necessary to complete the project and identifies the operations that control the project duration. To shorten the overall time, it is necessary to shorten the critical operations. For example, it would do no good to speed up the shaving or dressing; this would not shorten the overall time. On the other hand, spending a few minutes more over the first cup of coffee or reading the newspaper while waiting for breakfast to be ready will not delay the overall job.

OUTLINE OF STEPS IN USING CPM

In using CPM, we separate the *planning* of a job from its *scheduling*. Briefly, the steps involved are as follows:

1. Analyze the project. Determine the individual tasks or *operations* that are required.

2. Show the sequence of these operations on a chart called a *network*.
3. Estimate how long it will take to do each operation.
4. Perform simple computations to locate the *critical path* (the chain of interdependent operations that determines the duration of the entire project). This step also provides other information that is useful in scheduling the project.
5. Use this information to develop the most economical and efficient *schedule* for the project.
6. Use the schedule to *control* and monitor job progress.
7. Revise and *update* the schedule frequently throughout the execution of the project.

These steps are the basic elements of the Critical Path Method. Each step will be covered in detail in the chapters that follow.

A valuable extension of CPM introduces the element of cost. Recognizing that the cost of each operation is usually related to the time for completing it, this method, called *Least Cost Scheduling*, develops a relationship between completion time and total cost for the overall project. This can be used to find the cheapest way to shorten or expedite the job or to locate the *optimum time—* the completion time for which total costs are at a minimum. Least Cost Scheduling is introduced in Chapter 9. The first part of the text deals mainly with manual (non-computer) methods. Use of computers is discussed in Chapter 12, and the problem of selecting a computer program is dealt with in Chapter 13.

ADVANTAGES OF CPM

Successful users of CPM have found that they can achieve real benefits from its use. A few of these are as follows:

Shows Relationships

The network diagram (Chapter 2) shows the relationships between the various jobs that go to make up the project, and it shows the *dependency* of one job on another. Thus, it provides a much better picture of the job than was possible by a bar chart or other scheduling device.

More Effective Planning

CPM forces the project manager to think the job through thoroughly to completion. It demands careful, detailed planning. Many users feel that this fact alone justifies the time spent on the system.

Pinpoints Problem Areas

Properly applied, CPM helps to identify bottlenecks and potential problem areas before they occur.

Improves Communications

As soon as personnel are trained in its use, CPM provides an easily understood, graphical model of the job. It also provides a ready frame of reference for discussion between the parties concerned, such as owner, contractor, engineer or architect, and materials suppliers. This makes for effective, timely communication on job progress and control.

Resource Allocation

Through CPM the planner can determine the most effective use of personnel, equipment, and other resources. Overtime can be reduced or confined to the jobs where it will do the most good. Undesirable peaks and valleys in manpower requirements can be leveled out.

Study of Alternate Courses of Action

A powerful use of the method is in providing management with a means of studying different courses of action; for example, contracting out certain work as compared to doing the work with company forces. This type of study is known as *simulation*. It gives management the basis for making an intelligent choice between alternatives.

Management by Exception

By identifying the critical operations, CPM focuses attention on those jobs that control overall completion time. Further,

CPM defines just how far each of the other jobs can slip behind schedule without affecting overall progress. This permits true "management by exception," since management can concentrate on key jobs. At the same time, limits are set up for the remaining jobs that must be met if the project is to be completed on schedule. Any slippage beyond these limits immediately signals the need for management attention.

A FEW LIMITATIONS

The listing of all the advantages possible from use of CPM should not blind us to its limitations. CPM is not a substitute for thinking or planning. On the contrary, to be successful, it requires the most careful, precise planning and demands that every step of the project be thought out more fully than ever before.

CPM requires the wholehearted support of management and active participation by the people who will direct the work. A common mistake is to turn over the scheduling to a staff "expert" or an outside consultant and hope that something worthwhile will result. The project manager and his staff must be a part of the planning process.

To obtain maximum effectiveness, CPM should not be confined to the preliminary planning stages of the project. It should be used throughout the job to monitor and control the work until completion. However, CPM itself furnishes only information. It takes prompt, effective action by *people* to keep the project on schedule and compensate for changes and delays.

A FINAL WORD

The principles of CPM are not difficult. Although both CPM and PERT are based on higher mathematics, only simple arithmetic is required to put them to use. However, CPM is something like swimming—it is easy, but it cannot be learned simply by reading about it. The reader is urged to work through the sample problems provided and then to practice the techniques on his own jobs—small ones at first—until they have become natural and easy for him.

Executives and others who are interested in the principles of CPM and its applications but not in detailed methods should still read Chapter 2, Network Diagramming, before turning to the chapters on applications, since the network is fundamental to an understanding of the method.

2

Network Diagramming

The heart of CPM, PERT, and similar systems is the *network diagram*. This is a graphical picture of the project, showing each step or operation, and the relationship between the steps. CPM can be a powerful management tool or a total waste of time, depending on the care with which the network is prepared. To draw a correct network requires thorough familiarity with the project, patience, and knowledge of a few simple rules.

There are two systems in use for drawing network diagrams. In the *arrow notation* each job or operation * is shown by an arrow, from left to right. In Fig. 2–1 the diagram means that

BUILD WALL   PLASTER WALL

Fig. 2–1

the operation *plaster wall* can not start until *build wall* is finished

The second system of notation uses a *circle* to represent the operations (Fig. 2–2).

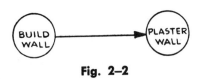

Fig. 2–2

Here the arrow is used to show that *plaster wall* must follow *build wall*. This notation is called *circle-line notation*.

---

* The individual tasks or elements that make up the project are called *operations* or *activities*. We shall use these terms interchangeably.

Each system has certain advantages; however, the arrow notation is the most commonly used and will be followed in this text.

Since we are using the arrow notation, we can also refer to the network as an *arrow diagram*.

RULES FOR DRAWING ARROW DIAGRAMS

1. Each operation is shown by a single arrow and must have definite starting and ending points. The tail of the arrow is the beginning of the operation, and the head of the arrow marks the end of the operation.

2. The diagram is not drawn to scale; that is, the lengths of the lines are of no significance (at this stage). It is, however, convenient to show the flow of work from left to right.

3. The relationship of the jobs is shown by the position of the arrows (Fig. 2–3). This means that b must follow a.

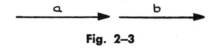

Fig. 2–3

Figure 2–4 shows that b and c must follow a but can be done at the same time. Neither b nor c can start until a is completed.

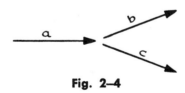

Fig. 2–4

Figure 2–5 shows that c cannot be started until both a and b are completed.

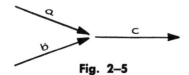

Fig. 2–5

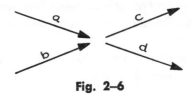

Fig. 2–6

Figure 2–6 shows that neither c nor d can start until both a and b are completed.

To summarize Rule 3: No operation can start until all the preceding operations have been completed.

4. In drawing a network for a real project, consider these questions:

 a) What operations must be finished before this operation can start?

 b) What operations can be done at the same time as this one?

 c) What operations can start as soon as this one is finished?

5. The network must be continuous with no gaps. This means that all operations (except the first ones) must follow some other operation, and all operations (except the final ones) must have at least one following operation.

6. *Dummy Operations.* The network in Fig. 2–7 shows that b follows a, and d follows c.

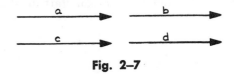

Fig. 2–7

Suppose, however, that b could not start until both a and c were completed.

The network shown in (A), Fig. 2–8, would not be correct. It shows that b depends on both a and c, but it also shows that d

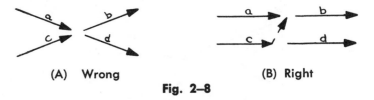

(A) Wrong   (B) Right

Fig. 2–8

depends on both *a* and *c* as well. To overcome this, we use a *dummy arrow* (broken line) as shown in (B), Fig. 2–8.

The dummy shows that *b* depends on both *a* and *c*, but *d* depends only on *c*. A dummy arrow used in this way is said to show *dependency*. Another use of the dummy arrow is in connection with numbering the network.

7. *Numbering the Network.* To identify each operation in the network, we may write the description of the work along the arrow, as shown in Fig. 2–9.

BUILD WALL ———▶ PLASTER WALL ———▶

Fig. 2–9

However, when doing calculations, it is convenient to use numbers instead of a lengthy description. For this purpose we add a bubble at each end of the arrow to hold a number (Fig. 2–10).

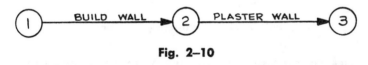

Fig. 2–10

Build wall may now be referred to as "operation 1–2," and *plaster wall* as "operation 2–3."

There are many systems for numbering the bubbles (their technical name is *nodes*), depending on how the computations are to be done. When the computations will be done by an electronic computer, the numbering system must suit the requirements of the computer. These systems are discussed in Chapter 13.

When doing the computations manually, we may number the network as we please, but the work will be easier if we follow the rule that the number at the head of the arrow should always be larger than the number at the tail. Thus, the numbers will always be increasing as we go through the network. Figure 2–11 illustrates this principle of numbering, which also satisfies many computer programs.

A good trick in numbering is to number by tens. In this way,

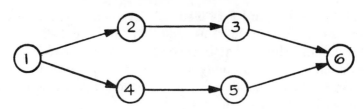

Fig. 2–11. Numbering the Network

if a new operation is added later on, the entire network need not be renumbered. In Fig. 2–12 operations 20–21 and 21–30 were added to the network.

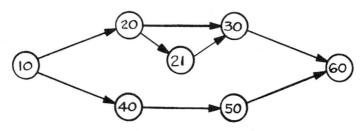

Fig. 2–12. Numbering by Tens

USE OF DUMMIES TO AVOID DUPLICATE NUMBERING

Consider the two operations shown in Fig. 2–13. These operations can be done simultaneously. However, with the arrows drawn as in (A), both arrows would be numbered 1–2; there is no way of differentiating between them.

If we speak of operation 1–2, we are not sure just which operation we mean. To overcome this problem, we introduce a dummy arrow as in (B), Fig. 2–13. Now we can speak of operations

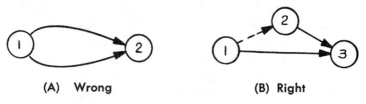

   (A)   Wrong   (B)   Right

Fig. 2–13.   Use of Dummy Arrows

2–3 and 1–3. Note that we have not changed the meaning of the diagram by adding the dummy; it is merely a device that avoids having two operations with the same numbers. Figure 2–13(B) does not mean that operation 1–3 will start ahead of 2–3. Actually, the diagram says that both 2–3 and 1–3 *can* start at the same time, and that both operations *must* be complete in order to reach event 3.

ACTIVITIES AND EVENTS

Each arrow signifies an operation or activity that takes a certain amount of time to complete. The circles or nodes also have a physical significance. They mark an instant in time when an operation is started or completed. Such a point in time is called an *event*.

Higher management is usually more interested in important events (which may represent the completion of major phases of the project) than in the specific operations connecting these events. In such a case, we may label the *events*, as well as the activities, as in Fig. 2–14. In PERT it is the events that are usually emphasized.

Fig. 2–14. Labeling Events

Now that we understand events as points in time marking the beginning or end of an operation, we can add one more rule for network diagramming, which will make our computations easier.

8. Always start a project with a single *event* and end with a single *event*. While it is usually easy to see how a project can start with a single event, sometimes there are many unrelated completion events. In this case, a final event—"project completed"—should be added, and the other "end" events connected to it by means of dummy arrows, as in Fig. 2–15.

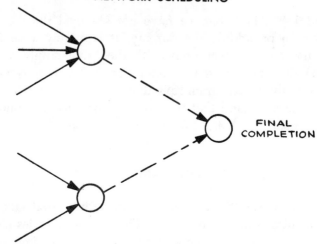

Fig. 2–15. Use of Dummies To Connect Final Events to a Single Ending Event

SUMMARY OF RULES FOR ARROW DIAGRAMS

We can now summarize the rules for preparing arrow diagrams:

1. Each operation is shown by a single arrow.
2. The diagram is not drawn to scale.
3. No operation can start until all preceding operations have been completed.
4. Consider the three basic questions:
   a) What jobs must precede this one?
   b) What jobs can follow this one?
   c) What jobs can be done simultaneously?
5. Every operation must have a preceding and a following operation, except the first and last.
6. Use dummies to show the correct dependencies between events and to avoid having more than one operation with the same set of event numbers.
7. Number the network in such a way that the numbers always increase as you go from the start to the finish.
8. Use only one starting event and one ending event.

USE OF BASE LINE

Frequently, a great many activities will start or "burst" from the beginning event. In this case, it is convenient to represent the starting event with a *base line* rather than a circle. The base line may be thought of as an expanded bubble. Figure 2–16 shows part of a network using a base line.

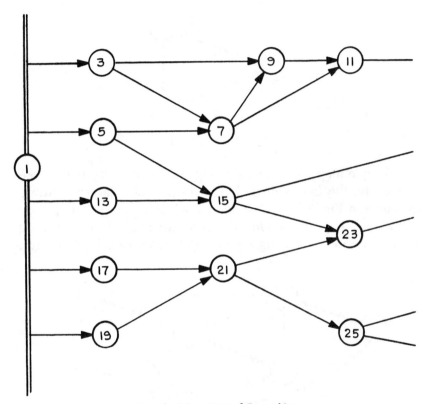

Fig. 2–16. Use of Base Line

ERRORS IN NETWORK DIAGRAMS

Two common errors in drawing network diagrams are *loops* and *incorrect dependencies*.

Loops

Figure 2–17 illustrates a loop. A little thought will show that this is an impossible situation. According to the rules we have established, *b* cannot start until *a* is completed, and *c* cannot start until *b* is completed. However, *a* cannot start until *c* is completed. Thus, none of the three activities can ever start or finish. Something is wrong with the thinking.

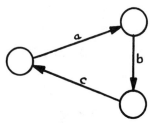

Fig. 2–17.   Loop

A simple loop such as that in Fig. 2–17 is easy to spot. More commonly, the loop will be buried in part of a larger network, as shown in Fig. 2–18. Here the cross-hatched lines form an unintentional loop. Observing the convention of always drawing the arrows from left to right will help to avoid this kind of error.

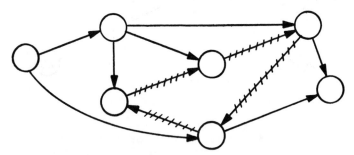

Fig. 2–18.   A Network Diagram with Incorrect Logic (Loop)

Incorrect Dependency

Another common error in drawing networks is *incorrect dependency*. What this means is best illustrated by an example.

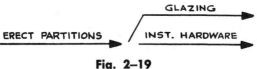

Fig. 2–19

Assume that in an office alteration project, the operations of installing hardware and glazing can be done after the partitions are erected. This would be shown as in Fig. 2–19.

Now, assume that the hardware is not on hand and must be ordered. To show this, another arrow is required: "deliver hardware." The tendency might be to show this delivery as in Fig. 2–20.

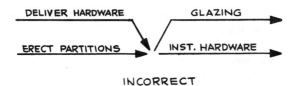

INCORRECT

Fig. 2–20. Incorrect Dependency

This, however, would be an *incorrect dependency,* since the glazing is not dependent on the hardware. To show the proper relationships, we must add a dummy, as shown in Fig. 2–21. Watch out for this common error when preparing a network.

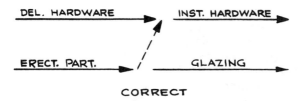

CORRECT

Fig. 2–21. Revised Diagram Showing Correct Dependency

THE NETWORK DIAGRAM AS A PLANNING TOOL

Drawing the arrow diagram completes the first phase of CPM. Many users of CPM feel that they get real benefit just from drawing the network—even if they go no further. Preparing the arrow diagram forces one to think through the job completely and determine just what the sequence of operations is to be. In addition, the diagram provides a readily understood picture of the project, which is useful for briefing new personnel; for client contact; and, generally, to facilitate communications.

PROBLEMS

Draw an arrow diagram for each of the following situations. Start with one node and end with one node. Assume that all operations can proceed simultaneously, except for the restraints given. Use dummy arrows only where necessary. Number each diagram, following the convention of having numbers increase through the network.

2–1. *A* must precede *B*.
B must precede *C* and *D*.

2–2. *B* and *C* precede *D*.
A precedes *B*.

2–3. *A* and *B* must precede *D*.
A must precede *C*.
D must precede *E* and *F*.
C must precede *E*.
E and *F* must precede *G*.

2–4. *M* must precede *N*, *O*, and *P*.
L must precede *O* and *P*.
N and *P* must precede *Q* and *R*.
O and *Q* must precede *S*.
R must precede *T*.
O and *Q* must precede *T*.

2–5. The diagram shown in Fig. 2–22 was drawn to satisfy the following conditions:
C follows *A* and *B*.
D follows *B*.
E and *F* follow *C*.
F follows *D*.
E and *F* precede *G*.
Find and correct at least three errors in the diagram.

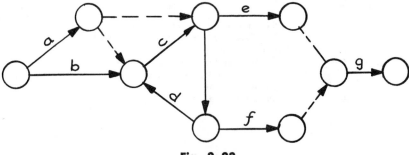

Fig. 2–22

2–6. Rita and Jack Stevens are planning to redecorate their finished attic. While Rita decides on the paint color and buys the paint, Jack will patch the plaster walls and ceiling. When this is done and the paint is delivered, Rita will start painting. As soon as Jack has finished patching the plaster, he will replace an unsightly broken window pane.

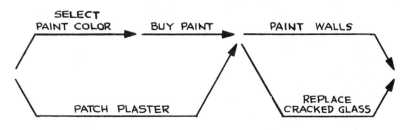

Fig. 2–23

The diagram in Fig. 2–23 shows the steps in this project. However, there is an *incorrect dependency* in the network. Redraw the diagram to show the correct network logic.

2–7. The following operations are involved in changing a flat tire on an automobile. Draw a network diagram showing these operations in their proper sequence. Do not consider any limitations on the number of people available to do the job.

Operation	Description
a	Take out jack and tools from trunk
b	Remove spare tire from trunk
c	Jack up car
d	Pry off hubcap
e	Loosen wheel bolt nuts with wrench
f	Remove nuts and store
g	Remove flat tire
h	Place spare tire on wheel

Operation	*Description*
i	Place nuts and tighten with fingers
j	Complete tightening nuts with wrench
k	Replace hubcap
l	Replace flat tire in trunk
m	Lower car and remove jack
n	Replace tools in trunk
o	Replace jack in trunk

3

How To Analyze
a Project for CPM

The preceding chapter dealt with the mechanics of drawing a network diagram to show the series of operations that make up a project. When it comes to breaking down an actual project into its individual tasks or operations, many other factors must be considered in addition to the rules for arrow diagramming. This chapter will discuss choosing the operations to be shown on the diagram, determining the amount of detail to be shown, and the special problem of operations that overlap each other.

ACTIVITY DEFINITION

What determines a single element or operation of a project? When should elements be combined and when should they be shown separately? There is no rule that will provide definite answers to these questions. In general, the activities used for CPM are much smaller and more detailed than work elements used in older types of scheduling. For example, "plumbing" is not satisfactory as an operation. Plumbing roughing must be installed before the walls are covered, and installation of the fixtures must wait until a later part of the project, after the walls are completed. Thus, plumbing must be broken down into at least two activities—"install roughing" and "finish plumbing." If the plumbing is a significant part of the job, further breakdown is necessary.

The following are some of the factors to consider when breaking down a project into its individual operations.

Physical Part

In the case of a construction project, it is logical to separate such different physical elements as roof, walls, floor, etc. Similarly, in planning a space rocket, the motor, guidance system, fuel tanks, etc., would constitute separate parts or elements.

Contractual Responsibility

It is frequently convenient to show as separate activities tasks that will be done by different companies. This is a help later in pinpointing responsibility and makes it easier to get estimates. As an example, if in installing a window, the frame is installed by one subcontractor, the glazing by another, and the sealer by a third, three separate arrows would be used to show the work. Other arrows might be required to show delivery of the various window items. Similarly, where tests, material approvals, or design checks are involved, it is essential to show them as separate arrows to emphasize the separate responsibilities involved. This principle may also be applied to different departments of the same company.

Trade or Skill Involved in the Work

A fundamental basis for breaking down the job is by the type of skill or craft necessary. Such distinctions are well recognized and form convenient work packages that will be familiar to anyone connected with the project. Separation by trade or skill is also useful when considering (later—during the scheduling phase) such factors as availability of manpower, workloads, level of skill, etc.

Location

Another factor to consider in making the breakdown is the location where the work will be performed. Thus, work done in the shop would be separated from that done in the field, since each of these is subject to different influences—shop work to the level of backlog work and field work to weather conditions, crowding, and availability of hoists and other equipment.

It may also be necessary to subdivide work done in different locations on the same site. On a large building, for example, the contractor may be pouring footings at one end of the site while still excavating at the other end. This introduces the special problem of overlapping activities, which is considered later in this chapter.

ACTIVITIES FREQUENTLY OMITTED

There are certain activities that are often neglected, since they may not show up in a conventional work schedule or cost estimate. Some of these are:

1. Time for taking bids and awarding subcontracts
2. Preparation of shop drawings
3. Review and approval by the architect, engineer, or owner
4. Submission of samples or catalog illustrations for approval
5. Material procurement lead times
6. Time for revising plans and specifications (in response to a change) or for issuing contract changes
7. Time for drying of plaster, curing of concrete, and other "natural" actions

Needless to say, omission of this type of activity will result in an incorrect arrow diagram.

DEGREE OF DETAIL

An important problem is to decide just how detailed the network should be. Several factors are involved.

Purpose

The first consideration is the purpose of the network. If it is to be used for preliminary planning, it can contain fewer items. On the other hand, if it is to be used for day-by-day control of the

project, it should be as detailed as possible. The situation is somewhat analogous to a cost estimate. When making a rough, preliminary estimate of the cost of a building, the estimator may use
an average cost of so much per square foot. For a detailed estimate he will measure the quantities of each item—excavation,
steel, concrete, etc.—and price each of them. In the same way,
the detail of the network should reflect its intended use.

Level of Use

Closely related to purpose is the *level* at which the diagram and
the resulting reports are to be used. In general, for reporting to
higher management, the diagram should be simpler and less detailed than a diagram for use at the field level.

Contractor vs. Subcontractor

In the CPM network for construction of a building, a general
contractor might show delivery and installation of a boiler as one
or two operations (arrows). On the other hand, the subcontractor
who will do this work will want to analyze it in detail. He will
need a complete arrow diagram for this one installation.

Degree of Importance

The extent of detail should also reflect—to some degree at least—
the importance of the activities to the overall project. In general,
critical and near-critical activities, or those that involve a high
level of risk, should be given the most detailed treatment. Minor
activities involving little or no risk of delay may be safely lumped
together. Since you do not know which operations are critical
until after you do the computations and locate the critical path, it
may be necessary to go back and reanalyze critical or near-critical
portions of the network, breaking them down in greater detail.

PYRAMID OF NETWORKS

For a large project it is often desirable to have several levels of
networks, as illustrated in Fig. 3–1. Under the "pyramid of net-

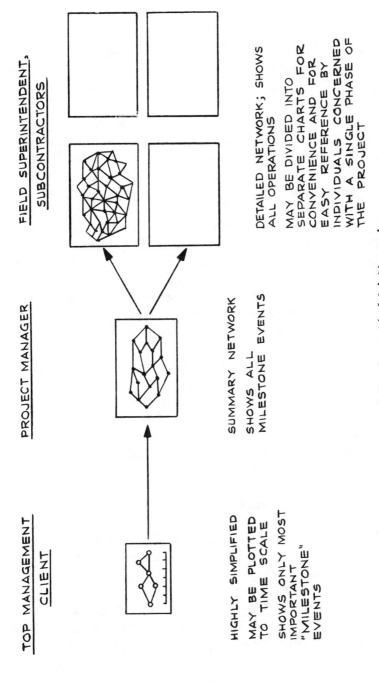

Fig. 3–1. Pyramid of Job Networks

works" concept, a detailed network forms the lowest level. This is for use by supervisors and subcontractors and shows each operation. It is better to prepare separate detailed charts for each phase of the project rather than to squeeze all the arrows into one huge chart. Each supervisor or contractor then has a chart showing his own phase. The set of detailed charts will have several hundred to several thousand activities.

The project manager is less interested in the details of each individual operation. His concern is with overall supervision and he must be able to view the entire project. This need is met by a summary chart having perhaps 100 to 300 arrows.

For presentation to a client or for use by top management, a highly simplified chart would be used. Since management is usually concerned with many projects, rather than just one, this chart presents only the barest summary of this project, showing the most important events. These might be completion of a building or other major element, delivery of important equipment, operational readiness dates, etc. Such important events are often called *milestones*. A summary chart of this type might have perhaps 30 arrows. Other refinements, such as drawing the chart to a time scale, are discussed in Chapter 11.

In summary, the degree of detail to be used depends on the purpose of the chart, the level at which it will be used, and the importance of the activities being analyzed. Where it is necessary to provide reports to higher levels of management, condensed or summary charts can be used. At the working level, it is always better to provide too much detail than too little.

OVERLAPPING ACTIVITIES

A frequent occurrence in actual projects is two or more jobs done in parallel, with one leading the other by a small amount. On a conventional bar chart this situation is shown by a series of staggered bars as shown in Fig. 3–2.

In CPM scheduling, the length of each arrow has no meaning. Each operation must be defined in such a way that it has a definite beginning and a definite ending point.

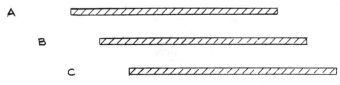

Fig. 3–2.   Overlapping Activities

A good example of this type of "staggered" work is construction of a pipeline.   For simplicity assume that the operations necessary to construct the pipeline are:

Excavate trench
Lay pipe
Backfill trench

Except for a very short pipeline, it is not reasonable to show these operations by a single chain of arrows, as in Fig. 3–3.

EXCAVATE TRENCH → LAY PIPE → BACKFILL →

Fig. 3–3.   Incorrect Representation of Pipeline Project

Actually, the trench would be excavated for a distance sufficient to lay one or more lengths of pipe.   Then, while the excavation continues, another crew would lay the first lengths of pipe. As soon as these are in place and connected, the backfilling operation could start.   On a conventional bar chart this situation would appear as shown in Fig. 3–4.

EXCAVATION

LAY PIPE

BACKFILL

Fig. 3–4.   Pipeline Project—Bar Chart

In CPM, construction could be shown by a series of parallel arrows, as in Fig. 3–5.   However, this is not strictly correct, since it does not show the fact that a definite amount of excavation must be completed before the pipelaying can start; and, similarly,

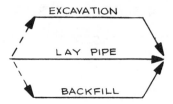

Fig. 3–5.   Pipeline: Operations Shown in Parallel

backfill cannot start until a given length of pipe is in place. We can deal with this problem in three ways.

Combine Staggered Operations

Where the operations are minor, and it is not essential to separate them, they may be combined and shown by a single arrow (Fig. 3–6). The overlap is then reflected in the time es-

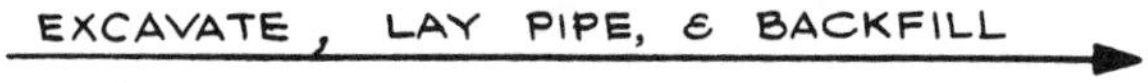

EXCAVATE , LAY PIPE, & BACKFILL

Fig. 3–6.   Combined Activities

timate for the combined activity. Thus, if there are two staggered activities, each taking 5 days, and the second activity cannot start until the first has proceeded for one day, the overall time estimate for the combined activity would be 6 days.

Use of a single arrow is very much a simplification and should be limited to minor activities; otherwise, the benefits of CPM planning are lost.

Detailed Breakdown of Activities

The most accurate way of handling overlapping operations is by breaking them down. For instance, in the pipeline example mentioned earlier, decide just how much of the trench must be excavated before the first length of pipe can be laid. Suppose this is 30 feet. The first operation will then be as shown in Fig. 3–7.

For brevity, we can call this operation "excavate trench #1."

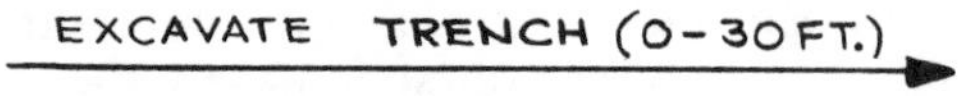

EXCAVATE   TRENCH (0 – 30 FT.)

Fig. 3–7

As soon as the trench has been opened for this distance, laying of the pipe can start. Meanwhile, excavation continues for the next 30 feet. This is shown in Fig. 3–8.

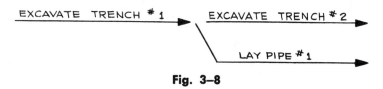

Fig. 3–8

Once a given length of pipe is in place, backfilling of the trench can start. This length of pipe defines the first pipelaying arrow, which for simplicity we have called "lay pipe #1." This arrow describes the laying of one length or two lengths of pipe, or whatever the planner feels is the necessary minimum.

The pipelaying can continue, however, but only if the next section of trench has been uncovered. This is shown by the dummy arrow from the second excavation arrow. The first attempt to show this relationship might appear as in Fig. 3–9.

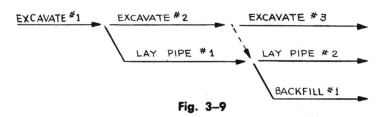

Fig. 3–9

Closer examination of Fig. 3–9 reveals an error: "backfill #1" depends on completing "lay pipe #1"—it is *not* dependent on "excavate trench #2." This is the "incorrect dependency" error described in Chapter 2. To show the correct dependency, we add another dummy, as in Fig. 3–10.

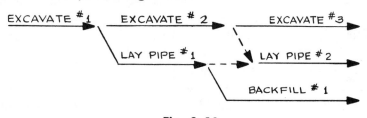

Fig. 3–10

The second "piece" of backfilling would follow "backfill #1" but only after completion of the second section of pipe ("lay pipe #2"). This is also shown by a sequence of arrows and dummies, as in Fig. 3–11.

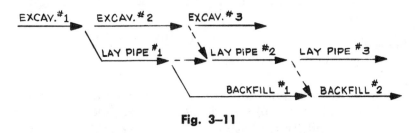

Fig. 3–11

The entire pipeline can be shown in this way, using a repeating pattern of arrows and dummies to show the proper relationships. This is illustrated in Fig. 3–12, which shows the complete project, assuming it to consist of five stages.

The detailed method is recommended whenever the most accurate picture of the work is desired. Use it when you are studying a small part of the network with the idea of improving the schedule. With this method it is important to define each operation carefully so that the network will give a precise picture of the sequence of construction.

Partial Breakdown of Operations

The detailed method of analysis, while accurate, is too cumbersome for most situations. On the other hand, lumping several overlapping operations into a single arrow is suitable only for minor operations. A reasonable compromise solution is to divide each activity into two or three arrows, as shown in Fig. 3–13. Here the first operation, "start excavation," corresponds to the first arrow in the detailed method. The second arrow, "complete excavation," represents the remainder of the excavation work.

Pipelaying is divided into three arrows. The first, "start pipelaying," is identical with "lay pipe #1" used in the detailed analysis. It represents the minimum length of pipe that must be laid before backfilling can start. The final pipelaying arrow, "complete pipelaying," represents that work that can be done only

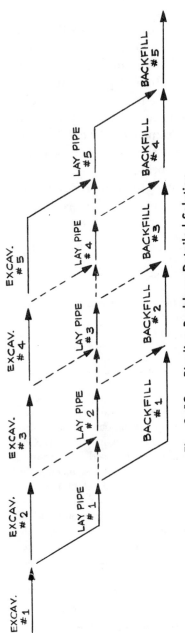

Fig. 3–12. Pipeline Problem: Detailed Solution

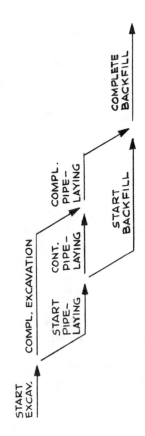

Fig. 3–13. Overlapping Activities—Partial Breakdown

after excavation is completed, while the middle arrow, "continue pipelaying," is the rest of the work.

Similarly, backfill is divided into two arrows. Here the bulk of the backfill operation is represented by the first arrow, while the second arrow, "complete backfill," shows only that last bit of back-filling that must be done after the last section of pipe is installed.

This method will give good results and is recommended where, as in the pipeline problem, the pattern of operations repeats itself with a series of identical operations. In some cases of overlapping activities, the repetitive elements are not the same—for example, pouring concrete on different parts of a bridge abutment. Here, while the pattern of work may be the same, the time for each element will differ. In such a case the detailed method is recommended.

PROBLEMS

3–1. You are planning construction of a plain (unreinforced) concrete foundation wall. The items of work involved are:

Excavate trench
Install prefabricated forms
Mix and place concrete
Concrete cures
Remove forms

The wall is 100 feet long. Approximately 35 feet of wall can be poured at one time. Although there is no limitation on the amount of form materials, only three crews can be used at any one time, as follows: One crew will be used for excavation, a second crew will be used for installing and removing concrete forms, and a third crew for mixing and placing the concrete. The forms crew can handle the removal of one set of forms at the same time that they are installing another set, if this is necessary.

Excavation and placement of concrete must proceed from one end of the wall to the other; forms can be erected in any sequence. Concrete must cure before the side forms are removed; the minor operation of re-moving the *end* forms before placing concrete for the next section of wall has been neglected for this example.

Draw a network diagram for this project using the detailed breakdown method.

3–2. Repeat problem 3–1, assuming that only one set of forms is available—enough to pour 35 feet of wall.

4

Time Estimates

PLANNING VS. SCHEDULING

In Chapter 1 we mentioned that in CPM we separate *planning* from *scheduling*. This is a key feature of the method. Planning is the process of analyzing the project, breaking it down into the steps or operations necessary for its completion, and finding the order in which these steps must be done. In CPM the results of the planning process are shown on the network diagram. The diagram also functions as an *aid* to the planning process, since it forces the planner to clearly define each operation and its proper relationship to all the others.

Scheduling introduces the element of *time*. First, the time necessary to accomplish each operation is estimated. With this information, you locate the critical path and then proceed to schedule the remaining activities. The result is a complete schedule for the entire project. This chapter will discuss the process of estimating the time for each operation in the project.

TYPES OF TIME ESTIMATES

Once the project has been divided into its elements, the next step is to estimate the time, or *duration,* of each operation. In general, estimates must be made for three types of operations.

1. The first type of operation involves labor, where the duration is usually determined from the number of man-days required

to complete the operation and the size of the crew that will be used. The formula is simply:

$$\text{Duration} = \frac{\text{Man-days}}{\text{Crew size}}$$

The effort (man-days) required to do the job depends on a variety of factors with which project managers and estimators are familiar, such as:

1. Type of work
2. Quantity
3. Working conditions
4. Location
5. Climate
6. Tools and equipment
7. Level of workers' skill
8. Degree of supervision

These factors all enter into conventional man-hours or man-days estimates and cost estimates. As a matter of fact, many of the time estimates for CPM can be obtained from the original cost breakdown prepared by the estimating department, provided the breakdown shows the labor effort (man-days or man-hours) required for each operation. In construction work most contractors have their own forms for making cost estimates. These can be easily modified for CPM use by adding columns for *crew size* and *duration*. An estimating work sheet of this type is shown in Fig. 4–1.

In using the work sheet, Fig. 4–1, the columns for crew size and duration may be filled in at the time the estimate is prepared, or this may be done later on during the detailed planning of the job. The project manager or job superintendent should participate in estimating these times, since he is the one charged with completing the project.

Columns are also provided on the work sheet for *identification numbers*. These are the numbers used on the CPM arrow diagram. The letter *i* refers to the tail, and *j* refers to the head of the arrow. These numbers are entered on the estimate work sheet after the arrow diagram is complete as a check that every item from the cost estimate has been shown on the network.

LABOR AND EQUIPMENT ESTIMATE SHEET

PROJECT		ELEMENT						SHEET	OF
DRAWING NUMBER OR SPECIFICATION REFERENCES			PREPARED BY					CHECKED BY	
Identification Numbers		Description	Quantity	Unit	Man-Days per Unit	Total Man-Days	Crew Size Equipment Required	Activity Duration (Work-Days)	
i	i								

Fig. 4–1. Work Sheet for Estimating Durations

Some care is necessary in using construction cost estimates for CPM job planning. To save time, an experienced estimator will usually lump together all items of a similar nature, having the same unit price, without considering the sequence of installation. For example, concrete of a given strength (say, 3,500-pound concrete) will appear as a single item, i.e., 40 cubic yards. However, not all of the 40 cubic yards will be placed at one time. For CPM each operation of placing concrete must be shown as a separate arrow. Thus, it is necessary to go back into the estimator's work sheets to find the quantity and time required for each "pour."

2. Operations that do not appear in the usual cost estimate, but which consume time, must be included. Examples are drying of plaster, curing of concrete, awarding of subcontracts, and the like. Also included are time for obtaining building permits, approval of shop drawings, and similar time-consuming items. Durations for these items must be based on experience and judgment, following the assumptions that will be outlined shortly.

3. The third classification is work done by some other agency, such as subcontractors, material suppliers, the owner, or architect. Ideally, major subcontractors should participate in developing the network. If this has not been done, it is a good idea to review the network with them at the time you ask for time estimates. A knowledgeable subcontractor can point out errors in the sequence of the work that others have missed. In any event, subcontractors and material suppliers should supply estimates for their own operations, whenever possible.

In connection with estimating times for material deliveries, a common situation occurs that seems to call for more than one starting event on the network. This is when the material delivery has a fixed date, rather than a known duration. This situation can be handled most simply by adding an operation, "deliver x," beginning at the starting event, whose duration will be the number of working days from the start of the project to the expected delivery date. Other fixed dates, such as access to the site, can be handled in the same way. A more extensive discussion of this situation is found under the subject of updating in Chapter 11.

No attempt should be made to introduce contract completion dates or similar targets at this time. This will avoid bias in the estimates. This and other rules for estimating times are discussed in the next section.

ASSUMPTIONS IN ESTIMATING DURATIONS

In estimating times for each operation, it is important to be as accurate and objective as possible. The following assumptions should be used:

1. Assume a normal level of manpower, equipment, or other resources for each operation. Ignore, at this stage, the effect of possible competition between two simultaneous operations for men, space, or other resources. Such conflicts will be considered later, after the computations and during the scheduling phase.

2. Consider only one operation at a time. For example, a sequence of work may involve delivery of equipment followed by its installation. The time estimate for installation should not be influenced by the possibility of a late delivery.

3. Assume a normal work day and work week. Do not consider overtime, unless regularly scheduled overtime is really part of the "normal" work day.

4. Do not consider known calendar completion dates. Otherwise, you will unconsciously try to adjust the durations to make them fit the time available. This will bias the estimates and defeat the purpose of CPM.

5. Use consistent time units. Any time unit (day, week, etc.) may be used, but the same unit must be used throughout. If days are used, they must be *either* work days or calendar days. Material deliveries are often quoted in calendar weeks, while work is usually measured in working days or weeks. If work days are the unit for a 5-day week, simply take 5 days for every calendar week, or 5/7 of the number of calendar days.

AVOIDING BIAS IN TIME ESTIMATES

The object of the time-estimating step is to come up with the most reasonable estimate of how long the operation should take.

To guard against bias, consider each operation by itself. It is also helpful when estimating times to skip around from one part of the network to the other, rather than to follow the operations in sequence.

CONTINGENCIES

No allowance should be made in the time estimates for contingencies such as strikes or floods. These factors cannot be predicted, and it is not reasonable to base a schedule on them. Weather delays are subject to a certain amount of prediction, however. If the project will take place during a rainy season, weather records can be used to determine the average number of dry days, and a factor can be applied to the time estimates for operations that are susceptible to delay by weather. On a long project, extending over more than one season, no such allowance should be made until after the critical path computations are completed (see Chapters 5 and 6). At that time it can be determined which operations fall within the period of bad weather.

UNCERTAINTY

There may be operations whose duration cannot be estimated with any degree of certainty. This might be the case in projects of an unusual nature, where plans are not firm, in research work, etc. For such situations simple probability techniques can be used. These are explained in Chapter 10.

As the times are estimated, they are entered directly on the arrow diagram, as shown in Fig. 4–2.

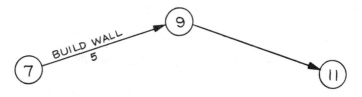

Fig. 4–2. Time Estimates Shown on Network

A dummy operation always has *zero* time; it is merely a convention used to show the correct relationships between the operations. However, it must be included in the computations.

PROBLEMS

4–1. In problem 3–1 the estimating department has furnished information as to the man-hours required for each phase of the work. Discussion with the estimator and project engineer gives the probable crew size. This data is shown in the following table.

Description	Man-Hours	Crew Size
Excavation	144	1 back-hoe operator 2 laborers
Erect forms	80	1 carpenter 1 helper
Mix and place concrete	72	6 laborers
Remove forms	16	1 carpenter 1 helper

The concrete must be allowed to cure for at least 1 day before the forms can be removed. All trades work an 8-hour day. Estimate the times (durations) for each activity shown on the network. Round off fractional days to the next highest full day.

5

Finding the Critical Path

In the previous chapters we have discussed the network and the duration of each operation; we are now ready for the next step: finding the critical path. The computations that identify the critical path will also furnish other valuable information that we can use in scheduling the project.

THE CRITICAL PATH

The critical path is what gives its name to the Critical Path Method. To show what critical path means, consider the network shown in Fig. 5–1.

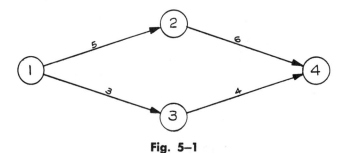

Fig. 5–1

There are only two possible paths through the network: 1–2–4 and 1–3–4. Adding the times along each path, we find that 1–2–4 takes a total of 11 days, while 1–3–4 can be completed in only 7 days. It is clear that the duration of the project represented by this network is controlled by the *longest* path (1–2–4). This is the *critical path*.

We may define the critical path as the chain of operations whose times determine the overall project time. This is the chain with the longest total duration. Operations on the critical path are known as *critical operations*. Any increase in the duration of a critical operation directly affects project completion time.

FLOAT TIME

Any operation not on the critical path (a non-critical operation) will have a certain amount of leeway or *float time* associated with it. Critical operations have *zero* float time. In the example of Fig. 5–1, operations along the critical path 1–2–4 cannot be delayed at all; they have zero float time. On the other hand, consider the path 1–3–4. If each operation along this path is started as early as possible, there will be 4 days of float time left between the completion of 3–4 and the completion of 2–4. Operations along 1–3–4 could be delayed a total of 4 days without affecting overall project time.

COMPUTATIONS

There are several methods for finding the critical path. The method we shall use in this chapter makes use of a simple work sheet, shown in Fig. 5–2. An alternate method, in which the

Project_____ Date_____ Sheet_____ of ____							
Operation							
i (1)	j (2)	Description (3)	Duration (4)	Early Start (5)	Early Finish (6)	Latest Start (7)	Latest Finish (8)

Fig. 5–2. CPM Computation Work Sheet

computations are made directly on the network diagram, will be presented in Chapter 6.

Drawing the network and estimating times call for considerable judgment and thorough familiarity with the project. By contrast, the computations are completely routine and can be delegated to a clerk (or, if desired, to a machine, such as an electronic computer). However, every manager who uses CPM should understand the computations—first, to be aware of just what the results mean; and, second, to be able to do his own computations when the situation demands a quick answer.

In using the work sheet, the information in columns 1 through 4 is copied directly from the network diagram. The starting and ending event numbers are entered in columns 1 and 2. Here *i* refers to the beginning event (tail of the arrow), and *j* refers to the ending event (head of the arrow). The operations are listed in numerical order, one to a line. The description is entered in column 3, and the duration, in working days or other units of time, is entered in column 4.

THE FORWARD PASS: EARLIEST START AND FINISH TIMES

Consider the simple network shown in Fig. 5–3. Each operation has been listed, in numerical order, on the work sheet of

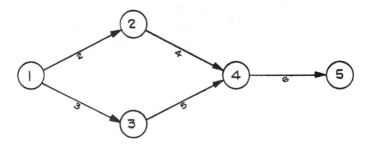

Fig. 5–3

Fig. 5–4, together with its duration. For simplicity, descriptions are omitted from this example.

Operation		Description (3)	Duration (4)	Earliest		Latest	
i (1)	j (2)			Start (5)	Finish (6)	Start (7)	Finish (8)
1	2		2				
1	3		3				
2	4		4				
3	4		5				
4	5		6				

Fig. 5–4. Work Sheet Showing Durations

Event 1 marks the beginning of the project. This may be at some time in the future or the past; but with respect to the *project*, it marks the beginning. We therefore assign all operations starting with event 1 an *earliest start* time of 0. This simply means that each of these operations can be started as soon as the project itself begins. Enter a 0 in column 5 next to operations 1–2 and 1–3.

The *earliest finish* time of any operation will be the *earliest start* time plus the operation duration. Thus, for operation 1–2:

$$\text{Early Start} + \text{Duration} = \text{Early Finish}$$
$$0 \quad + \quad 2 \quad = \quad 2$$

Enter 2 in column 6. Let us restate this principle as a rule.

Rule 1: Earliest Finish = Earliest Start + Duration

Using this rule, the earliest finish of operation 1–3 is day 3.

Consider now operation 2–4. This operation can start just as soon as operation 1–2 is finished. In other words, the earliest start of 2–4 is the same as the earliest finish of 1–2, which is day 2. Enter 2 in the earliest start column next to operation 2–4. Applying Rule 1, we compute the earliest finish of 2–4 as follows:

$$\text{Earliest Finish} = 2 + 4 = 6$$

In the same way, the start of operation 3–4 is controlled by the *finish* of operation 1–3 (day 3), and the earliest finish of 3–4 is:

$$\text{Earliest Finish} = 3 + 5 = 8$$

The work sheet now looks like that shown in Fig. 5–5.

Operation				Earliest		Latest	
i (1)	*j* (2)	Description (3)	Duration (4)	Start (5)	Finish (6)	Start (7)	Finish (8)
1	2		2	0	2		
1	3		3	0	3		
2	4		4	2	6		
3	4		5	3	8		
4	5		6				

Fig. 5–5

Coming now to operation 4–5, we find that it is preceded by *two* operations: 2–4 and 3–4. Our arrow diagram tells us that 4–5 cannot start until *all* preceding operations are finished. In the example, 2–4 is completed on day 6, but 3–4 is not complete until day 8, and hence 8 is the *earliest start* for the operation that follows (4–5).

We can state this as a rule.

Rule 2: Earliest Start = latest of the "Earliest Finishes"
of preceding operations

Using this rule, the early start of operation 4–5 is day 8, and its earliest finish is:

$$8 + 6 = 14$$

The work sheet now looks like that in Fig. 5–6. Since operation 4–5 is the final one in the project, we now know the earliest

Operation				Earliest		Latest	
i (1)	*j* (2)	Description (3)	Duration (4)	Start (5)	Finish (6)	Start (7)	Finish (8)
1	2		2	0	2		
1	3		3	0	3		
2	4		4	2	6		
3	4		5	3	8		
4	5		6	8	14		

Fig. 5–6

day on which the whole project can be completed. This is day 14—the *earliest finish* of the last operation.

The simple procedure we have described can be applied to any network, no matter how large or complicated. Remember

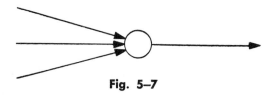

Fig. 5–7

that where several arrows come together, as in Fig. 5–7, you must be sure to use the *latest* of the *earliest finish* times for the preceding operations to determine the earliest start of the following operation.

THE BACKWARD PASS: LATEST START AND FINISH TIMES

We have now completed the "forward pass." This determines the earliest starting and completion dates for each operation. We shall now work *backward* through the network to find the *latest dates* by which we must start and finish each operation in order to complete the project in the shortest possible time. We have already determined that the earliest we can complete the project is day 14. To complete the project in as short a time as possible, day 14 must also be the *latest finish* of the final operation (4–5). Enter 14 in column 8 (latest finish) next to operation 4–5.

To find the latest start of this operation, we *subtract* the duration from the latest finish time. This is just the opposite of Rule 1.

Rule 3: Latest Start = Latest Finish − Duration

For operation 4–5 this is:

$$14 - 6 = 8$$

Enter 8 in the latest start column (Fig. 5–8).

Working backward through the network, if operation 4–5 is to start as late as day 8, both preceding operations must be completed by this date. Thus, the *latest finish* of operations 2–4 and 3–4 is the latest start of the following operation, 4–5, which is day 8. If there had been more than one operation starting at

Operation		Description (3)	Duration (4)	Earliest		Latest	
i (1)	j (2)			Start (5)	Finish (6)	Start (7)	Finish (8)
1	2		2	0	2		→4
1	3		3	0	3		→3
2	4		4	2	6	4	→8
3	4		5	3	8	3	→8
4	5		6	8	14	8	14

Fig. 5–8

event 4, the one with the *earliest* "late finish" governs. This is just the opposite of Rule 2.

> **Rule 4:** Latest Finish = earliest of the "Latest Starts"
> of following operations

Using Rules 3 and 4, we can work backward through the network, filling in the chart as we go. The latest finish of operations 2–4 and 3–4 is 8. The latest start of each of these is:

> Operation 3–4: Latest Start = 8 − 5 = 3
> Operation 2–4: Latest Start = 8 − 4 = 4

Operation 1–2 must be finished before the start of operation 2–4 (day 4), and 1–3 must be finished before the start of operation 3–4 (day 3).

Continuing, we find the latest starts for the remaining operations as follows:

> Operation 1–3: 3 − 3 = 0
> Operation 1–2: 4 − 2 = 2

The completed work sheet, showing earliest and latest times, is shown in Fig. 5–9.

Operation		Description (3)	Duration (4)	Earliest		Latest	
i (1)	j (2)			Start (5)	Finish (6)	Start (7)	Finish (8)
1	2		2	0	2	2	4
1	3		3	0	3	0	3
2	4		4	2	6	4	8
3	4		5	3	8	3	8
4	5		6	8	14	8	14

Fig. 5–9

Note that when we return to the starting event, the earliest of the "latest starts" is 0—the same as the earliest start of the first event. This is a check on the accuracy of the computations.

TOTAL FLOAT

At the beginning of this chapter, we defined float time as the amount of leeway or delay that could occur in any operation without affecting the overall project time. Actually, there are several kinds of float time, the most common being *total float*. Total float is the *maximum* time that an operation can be delayed without affecting the end date of the project. Total float is the leeway available if all the preceding operations are started as early as possible and all the following operations are started as late as possible. We shall use total float to find the critical path.

Total float for any operation is found by subtracting the earliest finish from the latest finish (or earliest start from latest start):

Total Float = Latest Finish − Earliest Finish
= Latest Start − Earliest Start

The same work sheet used for finding starting and completion dates can be used to compute total float. Figure 5–10 is the same

Operation		Description	Duration	Earliest		Latest		Float	
i (1)	*j* (2)	(3)	(4)	Start (5)	Finish (6)	Start (7)	Finish (8)	Total. (9)	Free (10)
1	2		2	0	2	2	4	2	
1	3		3	0	3	0	3	0	*
2	4		4	2	6	4	8	2	
3	4		5	3	8	3	8	0	*
4	5		6	8	14	8	14	0	*

Fig. 5–10. CPM Work Sheet with Columns for Total Float and Free Float

*Critical

as Fig. 5–9, except that additional columns have been added for total float (and for another quantity—free float—which will be explained shortly). To find total float, simply subtract the earliest from the latest finishes and enter the results in column 9. Subtracting the earliest from the latest starts will give the same results and can be used as a check.

IDENTIFYING THE CRITICAL PATH

To find the critical path, we recall that the critical path is that chain of operations whose durations determine the overall project time. Any delay in a critical operation will delay the project completion. Hence, critical operations always have *zero total float*. In Fig. 5–10 operations with zero total float (critical operations) have been marked with an asterisk. If these operations are now shown on the network diagram (i.e., by coloring or using heavy lines), they will form a continuous path through the network—the critical path. In Fig. 5–11 the critical path is shown by double lines.

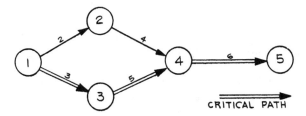

Fig. 5–11

Another way to think of the critical path is that, for a critical operation, the earliest start time is the same as the latest start time, and the earliest finish time is the same as the latest finish time.

CHARACTERISTICS OF THE CRITICAL PATH

The critical path must form at least one continuous chain from beginning to end of the network. There may be more than one critical path, and the paths may divide or branch out, but there can be no breaks or interruptions in the path; this would indicate an error in the computations.

For parallel critical paths to exist, there must be two or more parallel paths in the network having the same total duration, and this duration must be longer than that of any other path.

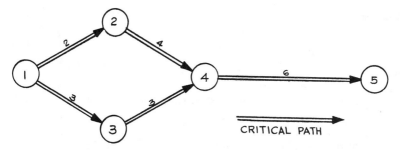

Fig. 5–12. Branching Critical Path

Figure 5–12 shows how a critical path can branch. The network is the same as that of Fig. 5–11, except that operation 3–4 has been shortened from 5 days to 3 days. This makes operation 1–2 and 2–4 critical and results in a branching critical path.

We have said that every operation on the critical path is a critical operation. Some confusion may result from use of the term "critical." In CPM an operation is critical if its duration directly controls overall project completion. Critical operations are not necessarily the most difficult or the most important operations in the project. They *do* require close management attention if the project is to be kept on schedule.

In most projects, including construction work, only about 10 to 20 per cent of the operations are critical. Identifying these operations focuses management attention where it is most needed and makes possible "management by exception."

FLOAT TIME; FREE FLOAT

So far, we have made use of the total float only to locate the critical path. However, knowledge of the total float for any operation is valuable scheduling information in its own right. For example, if a delivery is delayed, we can tell immediately whether the ensuing delay will affect project completion by considering the total float available to the affected operation.

A portion of the total float may also be available as *free float*. To utilize *total* float, the preceding operations must be started at their earliest start times and the succeeding operations at their latest start times. On the other hand, *free* float is the leeway available to the operation when *all* the activities in the chain are started as early as possible. Thus, an operation can be delayed to the extent of its free float without affecting any of the following operations, and all following operations may start at their earliest start times.

Free float is found by subtracting the earliest finish of the operation from the earliest start of the following operations:

$$\text{Free Float} = \text{Early Start of following operations} - \text{Early Finish of the operation}$$

In the example shown previously, only operation 2–4 has free float. Figure 5–13 is the completed work sheet showing both total float and free float. In general, free float is much less common than total float.

Operation		Description (3)	Duration (4)	Earliest		Latest		Float	
i (1)	j (2)			Start (5)	Finish (6)	Start (7)	Finish (8)	Total (9)	Free (10)
1	2		2	0	2	2	4	2	0
1	3		3	0	3	0	3	0	– *
2	4		4	2	6	4	8	2	2
3	4		5	3	8	3	8	0	– *
4	5		6	8	14	8	14	0	– *

Fig. 5–13. Completed CPM Work Sheet

The relationship between free and total float may be shown by use of a bar chart (Fig. 5–14), showing an operation plotted to some sort of time scale.* The solid portion of the bar (A–B)

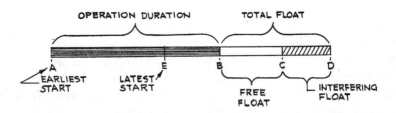

Fig. 5–14. Graphical Presentation of Total Float and Free Float

* John W. Fondahl, *A Non-Computer Approach to the Critical Path Method for the Construction Industry* (2d ed.; Stanford: Stanford University, Department of Civil Engineering, 1962), p. 29 and Fig. 6.

represents the duration of the operation. Point A is the earliest start, and Point B the earliest finish. The free float is shown by the white portion of the bar, $B-C$. Completion of the operation may be as late as Point C without affecting the schedule of any following jobs. Point C is also the earliest start of the following operations. The total float extends from B to D, which is the latest finish date. (The latest start time is shown as Point E; the distance $A-B$ and $E-D$ are both equal to the duration.)

The difference between total float and free float (shown as the cross-hatched area in Fig. 5–14) is often called shared or *interfering float*. If an operation uses some of its interfering float, non-critical operations that follow in the same chain will have to be rescheduled, even though final completion will not be affected.

In the example, Fig. 5–13, operation 1–2 has no free float; that is, all of its float is interfering float, which is shared with the following operation, 2–4. If 1–2 is delayed for 2 days, all of the float for *both* operations has been used up, and operation 2–4 must now be completed within its estimated time of 4 days if the project is to be finished on time. Use of free float does not require rescheduling of any of the following operations. In the example, operation 2–4 can be delayed by as much as 2 days without affecting the operation (4–5) that follows.

Once these simple characteristics are grasped, many uses for float time will become apparent in project scheduling and control. Some of these are discussed in the following chapters.

SUMMARY

The critical path is the chain of operations whose times determine the overall project time. Any operation not on the critical path has slack, or *float time*. To find the critical path by using a work sheet, duration is added to the earliest start time to find the earliest finish time, and the latest of the earliest finish times becomes the earliest start time of the following operations. In working backward through the network, we subtract durations from the latest finish times to find the latest start times, and choose the earliest of the latest start times as the latest finish of the preceding operations.

Free float is the amount by which an operation can be delayed without affecting succeeding operations; total float is the amount that the operation can be delayed without affecting *project* completion (some later operations will have to be rescheduled).

PROBLEMS

5–1. Given the network shown in Fig. 5–15, compute earliest and latest start and finish times, total float, and free float on the work sheet in Fig. 5–16. Locate the critical path and show it on the network.

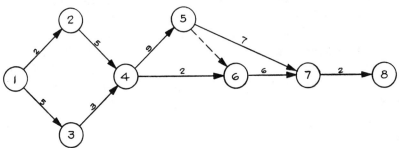

Fig. 5–15

Operation				Early	Early	Late	Late	Float	
i (1)	*j* (2)	Description (3)	Duration (4)	Start (5)	Finish (6)	Start (7)	Finish (8)	Total (9)	Free (10)
1	2		2						
1	3		5						
2	4		5						
3	4		3						
4	5		9						
4	6		2						
5	6		0						
5	7		7						
6	7		6						
7	8		2						

Fig. 5–16

5–2. The following list represents the operations involved in a plant maintenance project: removing and replacing a section of a pipe. Draw the arrow diagram for this project and compute the earliest and latest start and finish times. Tabulate the total float and free float for each operation and locate the critical path.

Operation	Description	Duration (hours)
A	Prepare materials list	8
B	Deactivate line	8
C	Procure and deliver pipe materials	160
D	Procure and deliver valves	120
E	Procure and deliver paint	16
F	Procure and deliver insulation	16
G	Erect scaffold	12
H	Remove old pipe and valves	36
J	Prefabricate pipe sections (except valves)	40
K	Install prefabricated pipe sections and valves	24
L	Start insulation of pipe and valves	24
M	Pressure test pipe and valves	8
N	Complete insulation	8
O	Paint insulation	16
P	Remove scaffold	4
Q	Reactivate line	4

RESTRICTIONS:

1. The scaffold is required for removing the old pipe but not for deactivating the line.
2. Operations *L* and *M* will be done concurrently and will precede operation *N*.
3. The pipe can be insulated after it is back in service.

5–3. Using the data of problem 4–1, find earliest and latest start and finish times and locate the critical path.

In problem 4–1, durations of fractional days were rounded off to the next full day. Does this result in an unrealistic overall duration for the project?

6

Computations on the Network Diagram

The computation method presented in Chapter 5, using a work sheet, is simple and straightforward and will serve for a network of any size or complexity. It lends itself to computing total float and free float and provides an easily read and understood tabulation of the results.

There are certain disadvantages to the method, however. The first is that all the data from the network must be copied onto the work sheet before computations can be started. This is a tedious process and is subject to error. Still another disadvantage is that to fully understand the meaning of the results, one must study both the arrow diagram and the computation sheet. Often, trying to locate a specific operation on both sheets at the same time slows down the use of the data.

There is one other limitation to this method. When a number of operations merge at a single event, the computation sheet must be scanned to determine which operation has the longest time and hence governs the starting time of following operations. If these merging operations are spread out over several computation sheets, it is easy to miss one.

For relatively simple networks, it is often faster and easier to do the computations directly on the network. Among the advantages of this method are:

1. Both the diagram and the day numbers appear on a single sheet and may be studied together. If the network is drawn on trac-

ing paper, a single reproduction step can provide copies of both the diagram and the computation to all concerned.

2. The step of copying information onto the work sheet is eliminated. This saves time and cuts out one source of error.

The basic principle of computing earliest and latest start and finish times on the network is simple. Add the times along each branch, stopping at a junction with another branch. When the times along all branches leading to a node are known, select the *largest* one and use this as the starting time for the following branches. The procedure is illustrated below. Note that, although event numbers are used here for reference, they are not essential and could be omitted.

Consider the network shown in Fig. 6–1. As before, all the starting operations begin at day 0. Add the durations along each chain of arrows, and note the cumulative total at the end of each arrow.

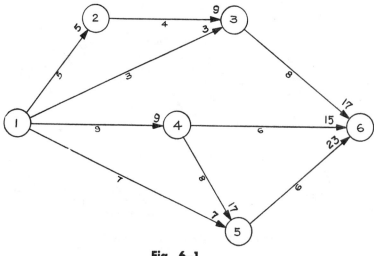

Fig. 6–1

First, add along 1–2–3 and note the total, 9. Since event 3 represents the junction of two branches, we must now return to event 1 and add along 1–3. With the total times for both branches written at the arrowheads entering event 3, we may take the largest total, 9, and continue adding along 3–6. We obtain 17 days for the total time entering event 6.

A similar procedure is followed through the rest of the network to find the maximum project duration, 23 days. This completes the "forward pass." A "backward pass" is now made, beginning with the last event and working back toward the start of the network.

With so many numbers on the network, it is easy to become confused. A simple notation system is required, using symbols to identify and organize each of the factors in the diagram. The symbols are shown in Fig. 6–2.°

As before, a line is used to identify each activity, with a circle to show each event. The duration (time) of each activity is

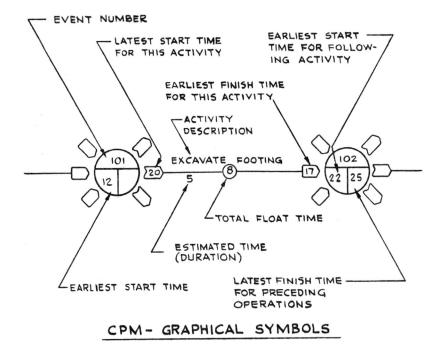

CPM – GRAPHICAL SYMBOLS

Fig. 6–2. Network Symbols for Computations on the Diagram

° These symbols are adapted, in part, from a system developed by Dr. Joseph J. Moder and Cecil R. Phillips, under the title "space symbols," copyright by Management Science, Atlanta, Inc., Atlanta, Ga. See Joseph J. Moder, "How To Do CPM Scheduling Without a Computer," *Engineering News-Record*, March 14, 1963, pp. 30–36.

shown above or below the arrow. The heads and tails of the arrows are enlarged to contain the earliest finish times and latest start times, respectively. The event bubbles are divided into three sections: The lower sections are used to carry forward the latest activity completion time and the earliest activity start times, and the upper half of the bubble is available for an event number, if desired. Finally, a small circle along the activity arrow is used to show total float.

Figure 6–3 shows the same example as Fig. 6–1, using the new symbols. Starting at event 1, enter a 0 in the lower left-hand sector of the event bubble. This is the earliest start time for the following operations.

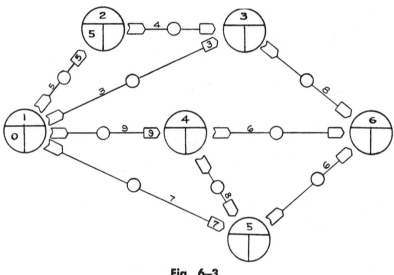

Fig. 6–3

Now for each arrow leaving event 1, add the duration to the earliest start time to find the earliest finish time. Enter this in the arrowhead pointing toward the right. For operation 1–2 this would be:

$$0 + 5 = 5$$

If there is only one arrowhead entering an event, enter the earliest finish from the arrowhead into the left-hand sector of the bubble. This is then used as the earliest starting time for the following operations.

Where several arrows meet at a node, select the one with the *largest* time (latest of the early finish times) and enter this in the following event. This is then used as the early start time of the following operations.

This procedure is used throughout the network until the last event is reached. The earliest time of the last event is day 23. This completes the forward pass and is shown in Fig. 6–4.

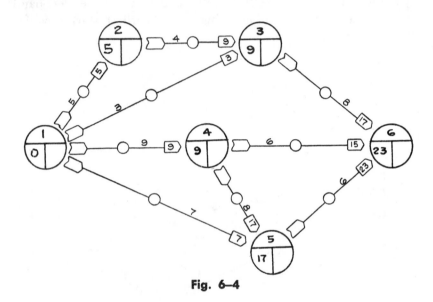

Fig. 6–4

THE BACKWARD PASS

To find the latest start and finish times, we now perform the backward pass. Since day 23 is the earliest possible day by which the last event can be reached, we enter it in the right-hand sector of the bubble 6 as the latest finish time. This day will be the latest finish of all the operations that merge at event 6.

Now *subtract* the durations from the latest finish time to determine the latest start time, and enter these in the *tail* of the arrow. For example, for operation 3–6:

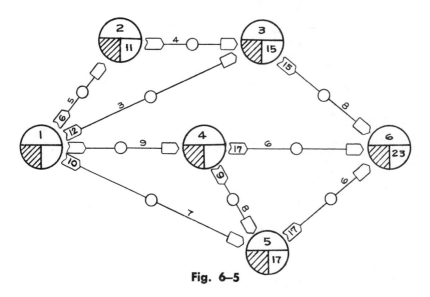

Fig. 6–5

$$23 - 8 = 15$$

This is shown in Fig. 6–5. (To avoid confusion when explaining the backward pass, the forward pass computations have been omitted from Fig. 6–5. The spaces where they would normally appear have been shaded in.)

Where several arrow tails "burst" from a single event, select the one with the *smallest* time (earliest of the late finish times) to enter in the right-hand sector of the bubble. Figure 6–6 shows a portion of the network at event 4. Here the smallest figure is 9; this is entered in the right-hand (latest time) sector. This is now used as the latest finish time for operation 1–4. Note that it is quite possible for the latest start of an operation to be a

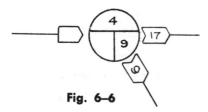

Fig. 6–6

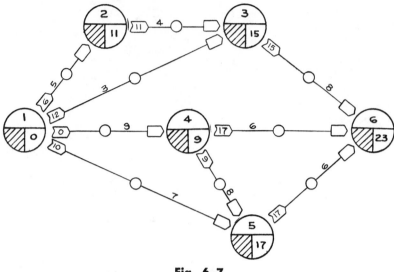

Fig. 6–7

higher number (later time) than its earliest finish, as for example in operations 1–3 and 1–5.

In the same way, we work backward through the network and find the earliest of the latest finish times at event 1 to be 0, which checks our computations. Figure 6–7 shows the network at this point, with the forward pass symbols omitted for clarity.

TOTAL FLOAT

To compute total float, recall that total float for any operation is equal to the difference between the latest and the earliest finish. With the symbols we have chosen, the earliest finish is

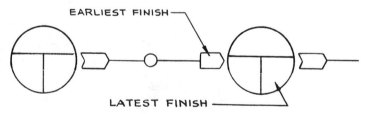

Fig. 6–8. Determining Total Float

shown in the arrowhead, and the latest finish is shown in the right-hand sector of the bubble, as in Fig. 6–8.

Subtract the earliest finish from the latest finish, and enter the total float in the small circle provided along each activity arrow. As always, any activity with zero float is a critical activity. These activities will form a continuous chain through the network—the critical path.

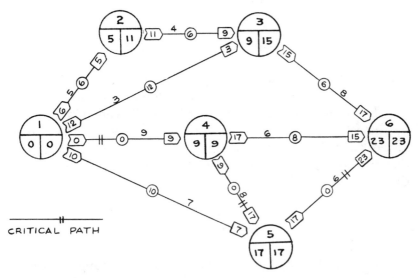

Fig. 6–9. Completed Network Using Graphical Symbols

Figure 6–9 shows the completed network with all computations, total floats, and the critical path.

No provision was made for showing free float, as this additional number would make the diagram too confusing. However, free float is easily computed, if desired. Simply subtract the earliest completion time (arrowhead) from the earliest start time (left-hand sector) of the following event bubble, as shown in Fig. 6–10.

Computations on the network are particularly convenient when only the forward pass is required. This may be the case when several methods of doing the work are being compared to see which will permit completion within the time available. It

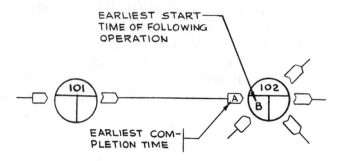

FREE FLOAT = B - A

Fig. 6–10.   Computing Free Float

is often possible to complete the forward pass in less time than it would take to copy the network data onto a work sheet.

When using this method, the results of the computations may be shown on a tracing of the network. Calendar dates can be added above the bubbles representing key events. Each print then provides both the network and the computations on a single sheet.

OTHER METHODS

There are other methods or routines for performing CPM computations, including a graphical method using strips of paper cut to length to represent each operation.[*] There is also a mechanical device available to accomplish the same purpose. The two methods presented in this text—work sheet method and network method—are considered the most practical for manual use and also for learning the method prior to using a computer.

SUMMARY

Computations may be done directly on the network, using special symbols to show earliest and latest start and finish times.

---

[*] David F. Sampsell, Lt. (jg), C.E.C., U.S.N., "A Graphical PERT Analog," *The Military Engineer*, No. 367 (Sept.–Oct., 1963), 321.

The computations are similar to those on a work sheet: durations are added to the earliest starting times when working forward through the network, and subtracted from the latest finish times when performing the "backward pass." This procedure is often faster and less prone to error than the work sheet method, and is particularly recommended for small networks.

PROBLEMS

6–1. Solve problem 5–1 using the symbols shown in this chapter.

6–2. Solve problem 5–2 using the symbols shown in this chapter.

6–3. Solve problem 5–3 using the symbols shown in this chapter.

7

Applications of CPM

Finding the critical path is a fundamental step in CPM planning. We have seen that this step gives us the "time boundaries" —the earliest and latest starting and finish times—as well as the float time. This and the next two chapters will discuss how this information can be put to use.

This chapter considers basic applications of CPM in such vital areas as scheduling, shortening a project, and determining the effects of changes and delays. Chapter 8 will show how CPM can help in the problem of assigning men, equipment, or other resources; and Chapter 9 will present a systematic method of shortening a project by reducing or "crashing" its critical operations.

DETERMINING PROJECT DURATION

The simplest and most obvious use of CPM is to find out just how long the project will take. The project duration can then be compared with the scheduled completion date, if any, to see whether or not it is acceptable. If the completion date is unsatisfactory, replanning may be required in order to shorten the job. Even if the schedule is acceptable, further changes may be made to reduce costs, even out manpower requirements, or accomplish other improvements. In all of these, CPM is a vital planning tool.

A rough, preliminary CPM computation during the bidding

stage will show the contractor whether he can meet contract completion without incurring expensive overtime. Similarly, an owner can use CPM to test the completion date that he has specified, since an unreasonable date will result in higher bids.

SCHEDULING

As previously stated, CPM separates *planning* from *scheduling*. In the planning stage, the sequence of operations is determined. In scheduling, actual dates are selected for each operation. If the completion date determined by the critical path computations is satisfactory, we may proceed to schedule the project. Starting and completion dates for critical activities are fixed by the CPM analysis. It is only necessary to convert from day numbers, produced by the CPM computations, to calendar dates. This procedure is facilitated by the use of a *job calendar*. This consists of an ordinary calendar, on which working days are numbered consecutively, omitting weekends and holidays. Figure 7–1 illustrates part of a job calendar for a major project.

NOV.					19X2	
S	M	T	W	T	F	S
	1 183	2 HOL	3 184	4 185	5 186	6
7	8 187	9 188	10 189	11 190	12 191	13
14	15 192	16 193	17 194	18 195	19 196	20
21	22 197	23 198	24 199	25 HOL	26 200	27
28	29 201	30 202				

Fig. 7–1. Job Calendar

Meaning of Day Numbers

A word is in order at this point regarding the physical meaning of a day number. "Day 12" means the *end of the normal work period* on that day. Thus, if an operation is scheduled for completion on day 12, it has the full day's working time in which to be finished.

We have assumed that all operations that could begin at the start of the project were started on "day 0." This really means the *end* of "day 0," or, as a practical matter, the morning of the first working day. The end of the first working day is *day 1*. If the CPM computations show that an operation has an earliest *start* of day 5, it cannot actually start until the *end* of day 5 or the morning of *day 6*. If it has a *finish* of day 5, on the other hand, it need not be completed until the end of the working day (day 5).

To summarize the above convention, the day number represents the end of the working period on that day. A convention of this kind, while arbitrary, is essential in order to obtain consistent results.

Use of Float Time

In scheduling the non-critical activities, the planner is at liberty to shift their starting and completion dates as he pleases— within the allowable float time. Note, however, that when float (other than free float) is used on one activity, it is no longer available for the remaining activities in that chain.

Modified Bar Chart

In scheduling with CPM, a modified bar chart is helpful. This chart combines the features of the conventional bar chart with the advantages of the arrow diagram. Start by drawing the critical operations, since their starting and ending dates are fixed. Then add the non-critical activities, trying several positions until a satisfactory arrangement is obtained. In drawing this modified CPM network, the following symbols are used:

1. A solid line represents an activity or operation.
2. A wavy line indicates float time.
3. An extra heavy line indicates the critical path.

As usual, dummies are shown by a dotted line. The final chart is useful for display purposes, since its meaning is easily grasped by anyone familiar with the conventional bar chart. Figure 7–2 illustrates an arrow diagram and the modified bar chart based on it.

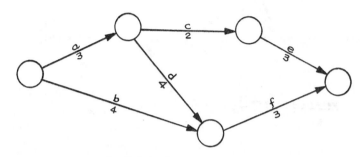

A. Original Arrow Diagram

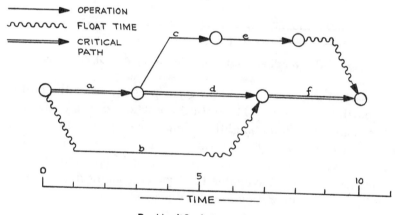

B. Modified Bar Chart

Fig. 7–2

For monitoring and reporting job progress, actual progress is shown alongside the planned lines, using a contrasting color or pattern. A vertical line of the same contrasting color shows the date of the report with which progress to date can be compared. Various types of colored and patterned tapes are available, which produce neat results with little effort. Figure 7–3 is the modified

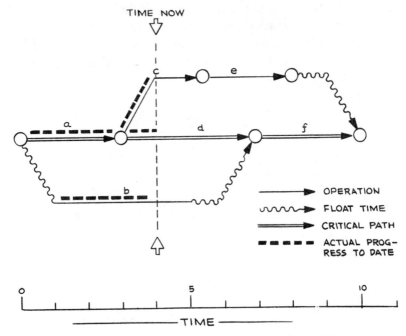

Fig. 7–3. Modified Bar Chart Showing Actual Progress

bar chart of Fig. 7–2(B), showing job progress as of the end of the fourth time period. The critical operation, *d,* is on schedule. Operations *c* and *b* are slightly behind schedule. In the case of operation *b,* this is not yet serious because there is ample float time (shown by the wavy line). In the case of operation *c,* there is sufficient float time available to absorb the slight delay. However, the start of operation *e* will be delayed.

SHORTENING A PROJECT

If a projected completion date is not acceptable, there are basically three ways of shortening the project:

1. One way is to replan the project, using different methods. For example, a complete design change may be called for, such as a switch from steel to concrete or vice versa.

2. The second approach is to replan the sequence of opera-

tions so that operations that formerly were in series are now done in parallel. In general, the more operations that are paralleled, the greater the attendant *risk*. For example, in designing a missile system, it is logical to design the launching facilities after plans for the missile are complete. This is shown in Fig. 7–4.

DESIGN MISSILE   DESIGN LAUNCHING FACILITIES

Fig. 7–4. Operations in Series

Under pressure to complete the system as fast as possible, these two operations might be done in parallel. Of course, in this case, design of the launching facilities will be based only on a general idea of the missile characteristics, and there is a definite risk that the launching facilities may not match the final missile configuration (Fig. 7–5).

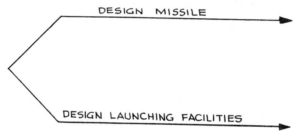

Fig. 7–5. Operations Paralleled

3. The third way of shortening is to apply additional resources (manpower, equipment, money) to the project to speed it up. Knowledge of the critical path makes it possible to concentrate this extra effort where it will pay off—on the critical jobs. In cases where additional personnel cannot be used, overtime is often employed to speed up a job or to make up lost time. Usually, the tendency is to work the entire project on overtime. It should be clear, however, that overtime (or any other form of extra effort) applied to non-critical operations is a *waste of money*, since shortening these jobs does *not* affect overall project completion times. On the other hand, a relatively small additional expenditure for overtime on a critical operation, or to expedite a critical delivery, can shorten the project considerably.

TRADE-OFF OF RESOURCES

In some cases it may be possible to transfer men, equipment, or other resources from a non-critical to a critical operation. This procedure can sometimes be used to shorten a project at little or no cost. Trade-offs of this kind will lengthen the non-critical operations, and the network computations should be repeated to make sure that, in lengthening, a new critical path has not been introduced.

In the network of Fig. 7–6 the two parallel chains represent work done at two different locations: Site A and Site B. Although similar skills are required at each site, the two locations are remote from each other so that it is not feasible to shift men back and forth once work has started. Initial planning for the project assumed a five-man crew for each site (See Table 7-1).

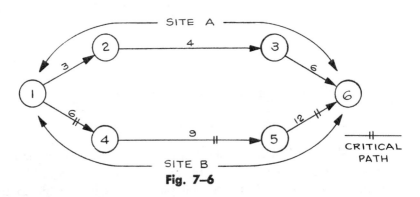

Fig. 7–6

The critical path is made up of the work at Site B (operations 1–4, 4–5, and 5–6). To shorten the project, we must reduce the time for these operations. One way to do this might be to hire additional men. Instead of this, we might use a smaller crew at Site A and put the man thus released to work on the critical operations at Site B. The operations at Site A would take longer, of course, but since considerable float time is available, these operations can be extended without becoming critical.

Suppose, for example, that we use a four-man crew at Site A and add one man to the crew at Site B. Table 7–1 shows the effect of these changes. By trading off one man from the non-

TABLE 7–1

	Opera-tion	Original			Revised		
		Man-Days	Crew Size	Dura-tion	Crew Size	Dura-tion	Man-Days
Site A	1–2	15	5	3	4	4	16
	2–3	20	5	4	4	5	20
	3–6	30	5	6	4	8	32
Site B	1–4	30	5	6	6	5	30
	4–5	45	5	9	6	8	48
	5–6	60	5	12	6	10	60
Total man-days		200					206

critical operations at Site B, we have reduced the overall project time from 27 to 23 days. The revised network diagram (Fig. 7–7) shows that there is still some float time left on the upper path.

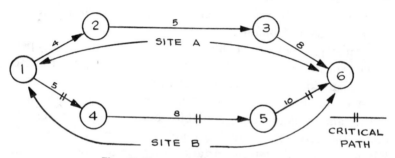

Fig. 7–7. Revised Durations

The revised schedule (Table 7–1) shows an increase in the effort (man-days) required to complete the project and hence an increase in the project cost. However, this is an increase of only 6 man-days compared to an additional 23 man-days that would have been required if the five-man crew had been retained at Site A and a sixth man hired for Site B in order to shorten the project.

This example has purposely been simplified in order to illustrate the principle of trading off resources from a non-critical to a critical operation. In practice, when scheduling manpower, machines, or similar resources, one must also consider the total number required each day compared to the number available on that day. This kind of scheduling is the subject of Chapter 8.

STRETCH-OUT OF NON-CRITICAL OPERATIONS

At the time the network was prepared, a certain level of resources was assumed for each operation. Once a satisfactory project duration has been reached, operations with large amounts of float time should be studied to see if costs can be reduced by *decreasing* the resources used. As an example, procurement items with large amounts of float time suggest the possibility of reducing costs by taking bids from additional vendors. Perhaps a supplier with a low price, who was previously ruled out because of a long delivery time, can now be considered. Certain items can be ordered from a manufacturer's warehouse, instead of from a dealer, at considerable savings. In other cases, suppliers may be able to offer discounts, if they can be given enough additional time to permit them to schedule their fabrication in the most efficient manner.

Similarly, where large float times are available, cheaper but slower construction techniques can be substituted for those originally planned. Perhaps it had been planned to rent an expensive piece of equipment for a certain operation. If CPM analysis shows ample float time available, eliminating this rental and doing the job with available equipment should be considered. Expensive means of transportation such as air freight should be eliminated for the non-critical items, and advantage should be taken of quantity carload shipments for some materials.

SCHEDULING OF MATERIAL DELIVERIES

An important use of CPM is in scheduling material deliveries. Materials must be on the job when needed. On the other hand, too early deliveries present problems of storage, damage, and pilferage, especially on a crowded construction site. With a precise schedule developed by CPM analysis, materials can be scheduled to arrive within a short time before they are needed. At the same time, the schedule will also show when orders must be placed for long lead-time items to insure on-time deliveries.

DETERMINING THE EFFECTS OF DELAYS

Use of CPM does not stop at the planning stage, or when the schedule is complete. It is a valuable tool for controlling the project throughout its execution. CPM analysis can determine the effect of a delay in one or more operations on the job as a whole. In construction work, bad weather, strikes, material shortages, and late deliveries are an ever-present threat. When these or other factors cause a delay, it is important to assess its effect on job progress.

Study of the network will show which operations are affected by the delay. If they are non-critical operations with sufficient float time, the completion date can still be met. The CPM analysis will reveal which operations must be rescheduled. If a critical operation is affected, the analysis will determine just how late the job will be, or how much the remaining critical operations must be expedited in order to bring the job back on schedule.

EFFECT OF CHANGES

Changes, like delays, are the rule rather than the exception in many projects. Design revisions, unforeseen conditions, changes in the owner's desires—all contribute to changed plans. That changes in plans may result in increased cost is fairly well accepted. The effect on contract time is frequently a matter of contention between owner, architect, and contractor.

With a CPM network the effect of a change can be precisely determined. Perhaps more important, the network provides graphic proof of just why a time extension is or is not required.

CPM AS A TOOL IN DECISION MAKING

Another application of CPM is in the simulation of alternate courses of action. Various methods may be under consideration for accomplishing some phase of the project. CPM provides a "model" of the project that is useful in comparing these alternates. Examples of such choices might be:

1. Evaluation of proposals with different delivery dates.
2. Shall we do certain work ourselves or subcontract it?
3. Shall we hire additional personnel, work overtime, or subcontract?

In design, various materials present differing problems of delivery, fabrication, or erection times. Often, time is an important factor in the choice between materials or types of design. CPM provides an effective and realistic tool to aid in decisions of this type.

SUMMARY

This chapter has dealt with some of the basic applications of the Critical Path Method. Once the computations are complete, the project duration is known. If this is satisfactory, a calendar date schedule can be set up. If the project must be shortened, knowledge of the critical path permits the planner to do so by changing the project design or methods, by paralleling operations, or by applying additional resources to the critical operations. Trading off resources from non-critical to critical operations can also be used to shorten the project. When scheduling, reducing the resources assigned to non-critical operations (stretch-out) can be considered to cut costs, and deliveries can be properly timed.

During the execution of the project, the network and CPM analysis permit assessing the effect of delays and changes on job progress and schedules. Finally, CPM studies can be used to simulate and compare alternate courses of action and aid in management decisions.

PROBLEMS

7–1. A project is scheduled to begin on October 25 of the current year.

    a) Prepare a job calendar, assuming that the project will work a 5-day week, and that Election Day and Thanksgiving will be observed as holidays. The job is expected to last for about 5 to 6 weeks.

    b) One portion of the site will not be available until November 12. To what day number does this correspond?

    c) A delivery is scheduled for November 15. If there are no other operations that must precede this delivery, what duration is used on the arrow showing this delivery?

7–2. In the project shown in Fig. 7–8, *A* and *B* represent deliveries of two important pieces of equipment. Bids were taken from three different manufacturers for each item, with results as follows:

ITEM A			ITEM B		
Vendor	Price ($)	Delivery (days)	Vendor	Price ($)	Delivery (days)
X	1,000	35	M	600	45
Y	1,250	23	N	950	25
Z	1,600	18	P	975	30

If the durations of the other operations are as shown in the arrow diagram, which vendor should be selected for each of the two equipment deliveries, *A* and *B*, in order to finish the project as soon as possible, but without incurring any avoidable extra costs?

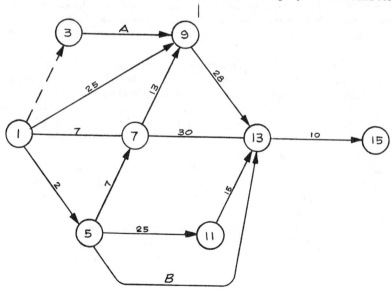

Fig. 7–8

7–3. Use the same data as in problem 5–2.

a) An alternate quotation for the valves will reduce the delivery time from 120 hours to 80 hours, at a slightly higher price. Is this advantageous?

b) During the course of the work, word is received that the delivery of the insulation will be delayed by 3 working days (24 hours). By how much will the overall project be delayed?

c) A crew of four men is assigned to erect the scaffold and remove the old pipe. Two of the men are called away for an emergency job elsewhere. Assuming that each of these two operations will now take twice as long as originally estimated, what is the effect on overall completion?

d) Plant management desires to keep the old line in operation as long as possible. What is the latest time that the deactivation operation should start, in order not to delay the job, but allowing an 8-hour "cushion" for unexpected delays or holdups in the deactivation?

e) If there are no delays in the execution of the project, what is the earliest time that the line can be back in operation?

f) During the final pressure test, a leak is found at one valve connection. If repairs will take 2 working days (16 hours), what will be the effect on final completion time? *Note:* A complete pressure test must be made following the repair.

7–4. The network shown in Fig. 7–9 represents a simplified plan for construction of a building. You are the electrical subcontractor and are involved only with operations 9–11, 19–21, and 25–27, shown by heavy lines. The General Contractor has prepared the arrow diagram and has told you that he intends to start each of his operations as early as possible.

In scheduling this job, you would like to work continuously, with as few interruptions as possible. This would avoid lost time when men are brought in for a time, then taken off the job, and then brought back again. After some discussion, the G.C. agrees to modify his plans in order to let you schedule your work at any time you please, as long as you do not delay any operation on the critical path, and as long as operation 21–23, which affects several trades, is completed no later than day 28.

In studying the network, you feel that while the G.C. may be successful in completing most operations by their earliest finish date, operation 3–9 will very probably be delayed. You estimate that this operation may be as much as 2 weeks late.

Schedule each of your operations so as to have a minimum of interruptions, in keeping with the other factors listed above.

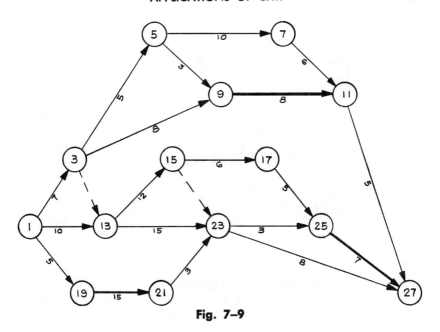

Fig. 7–9

8

Allocating Manpower and Other Resources

Every project requires resources for its accomplishment. These include space, equipment, funds, and, of course, manpower. In Chapter 7 we discussed the possibility of speeding up completion of a project by shifting resources from non-critical to critical operations. Let us now consider how CPM may be used in the general problem of scheduling and allocating these resources.

In preparing the arrow diagram, we assumed a "normal" level of resources and ignored the effect of conflicting demands for limited resources. Once the CPM analysis is completed, we must consider these limitations and their effect on our schedules.

MANPOWER LEVELING

Manpower is an important resource that is usually limited in some degree. We will use *manpower leveling* to illustrate the general procedure for allocating any resource.

Avoiding Fluctuations

In any project it is desirable to avoid sharp fluctuations in manpower requirements. Recruiting, hiring, and training personnel are costly and time-consuming; and once hired, men cannot always be let go and then rehired in response to varying needs. This is especially true where men are hired for a fixed period of time, such as at remote locations.

Although desirable, it is not always possible to maintain a constant work force, particularly in one-time jobs. However, it is feasible to achieve a smooth buildup of manpower followed by

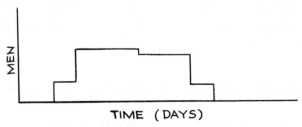

TIME (DAYS)

Fig. 8–1. Manpower-Time Graph

a tapering off, with a minimum of fluctuations during the job. A typical manpower-time curve showing this scheduling goal is given in Fig. 8–1.

Limited Resources

A second problem of manpower (or other resource) scheduling is concerned with the limitations on the number of men available. It is frequently necessary to complete the job without exceeding a given number of men in each craft. This comes about because the additional men may not be available, or the cost of hiring and training them may be excessive, or because the working area may permit only a certain number of workers at one time.

Fixed Level of Resources

A third situation arises when it is desirable to do the job with a *fixed* number of men. This is the situation in any shop or office having a fixed number of men on the payroll. Obviously, it is desirable to keep these men fully employed as much of the time as possible.

CPM and Manpower Scheduling

These are the problems of resource scheduling: how to avoid unwanted peaks and valleys in manpower levels, how to complete the work with a limited number of men, and how best to utilize a fixed number of men to accomplish the work. CPM can help in each of these problems. Two methods are used—the graphical method and the work sheet method.

GRAPHICAL METHOD FOR MANPOWER SCHEDULING

To illustrate the graphical method, we will show how CPM can help to iron out excessive peaks and valleys in the manpower requirements. A chart, something like a bar chart, is the key to the method. The horizontal scale represents units of *time* (work days, weeks, etc.), while the vertical scale shows the number of men. Each operation is drawn as a rectangle or a series of rectangles whose height corresponds to the number of men needed for that operation and whose length is drawn equal to the duration of the operation (in the scale chosen). The duration is taken directly from the CPM network. For example, a job that takes two men 5 days to perform would be shown by a rectangle, two units high and five units wide, as shown in Fig. 8–2.

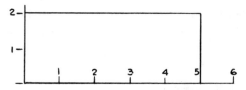

Fig. 8–2. Graphical Representation of a Single Operation

If the crew size varies, the job can be represented by a *series* of rectangles, as shown in Fig. 8–3. However, where the variation in crew size is minor, it is better to use a single rectangle with a height equal to the *average* number of men required.

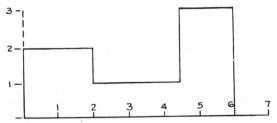

Fig. 8–3. Graphical Representation of an Operation Where the Crew Size Varies

To start the diagram, first plot the rectangles representing *critical operations,* because their position in time is fixed. Then lightly sketch in the non-critical operations above the critical operations. When all rectangles have been drawn on the graph, the topmost line of the diagram will show the total manpower required at any given time.

Study the diagram, and adjust the position of the non-critical operations—within the range of their available float time—to give as smooth a curve of manpower as possible.

The procedure is illustrated by the following simple example. The table following the diagram of Fig. 8–4 shows the duration of each operation as well as the size of the crew which the planner felt would be needed for each operation. After the compu-

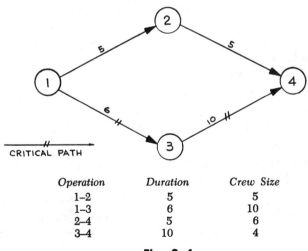

Operation	Duration	Crew Size
1–2	5	5
1–3	6	10
2–4	5	6
3–4	10	4

Fig. 8–4

tations are completed (in this case by adding mentally along each path as described in Chapter 6), the critical operations are plotted in order on cross-ruled paper in the manner described above.

As a first trial, the non-critical operations may be plotted to start as *early* as possible (Fig. 8–5). The resulting manpower

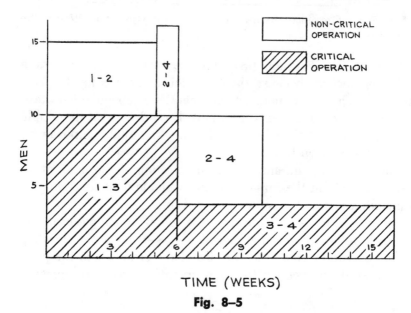

TIME (WEEKS)

Fig. 8–5

curve shows a very non-uniform use of manpower with a peak during the fifth week. This peak can be eliminated by shifting operation 2–4 slightly within its allowable float time (Fig. 8–6).

If a more uniform manpower curve is desired, both non-critical operations may be adjusted, as shown in Fig. 8–7. Note that the critical operations have not been affected, so that there is no change in project time.

This type of analysis can be made for the job as a whole, or for individual trades, particularly for those where the supply of skilled manpower is limited or where fluctuations in manpower are objectionable. The same approach can also be used for scheduling equipment (such as a crane) or any other limited resource.

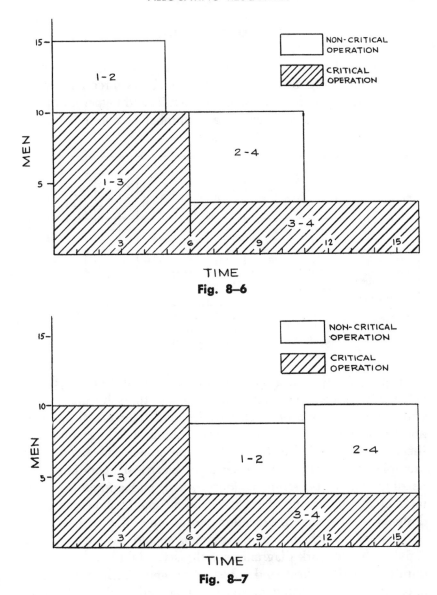

Fig. 8—6

Fig. 8—7

In some cases there may not be enough men (or other resource) available to complete the project within the planned duration. A manpower or resource study of the type shown will show the effect of this limitation on the completion date.

WORK SHEET METHOD

The second method of scheduling manpower uses the work sheet shown in Fig. 8–8. The illustration shows three labor classifications for each day (foreman, mechanic, and helper), but the form could be used to schedule any number of different trades.

| | | Crew Size | | Day or Week | | | | | | | | | | | |
| | | | | 1 | | | 2 | | | 3 | | | 4 | | |
Operation	Description	Norm.	Min.	F	M	H	F	M	H	F	M	H	F	M	H
Men Required															
Men Available															

F = Foreman   M = Mechanic   H = Helper

Fig. 8–8. Manpower Scheduling Form

In practice, related groups of operations would be scheduled on separate sheets (i.e., plumbing), so that the scheduler works with a limited group of related trades, and the work sheet does not become too cumbersome. The column headings on each sheet would be filled in to suit the type of work involved. For example, when scheduling a series of electrical operations, the headings would be foreman, journeyman, and apprentice. For tasks in an engineering office, the headings might show engineer, designer, draftsman, specification writer, etc.

To start the scheduling, the planner should have available a copy of the network diagram as well as the tabulation showing durations and earliest and latest start and finish dates. The operations may be listed in any order on the work sheet; however, it is recommended that they be listed approximately in order of their early start dates.

The operations should be divided into a series of convenient groups, and the groups should be scheduled in roughly the order in which they appear on the work sheet—by early start. Within each group, the critical operations should be scheduled first, followed by the non-critical operations in order of increasing float time.

ILLUSTRATIVE PROBLEM

We will illustrate the procedure with a simple example, shown in Fig. 8–9. In addition to the network diagram, we also need

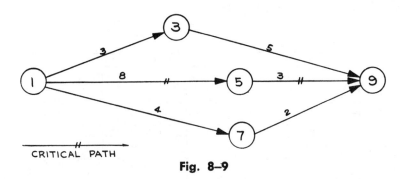

Fig. 8–9

the normal crew size for each operation. This is the crew size on which the planner based his estimates of duration. To simplify the presentation, we shall assume that only one skill or craft is involved in all the operations of the sample problem.

Operation	Normal Crew Size	Minimum Crew Size
1–3	4	2
1–5	4	2
1–7	2	1
3–9	3	1
5–9	2	1
7–9	5	3

We have also listed the *minimum crew size,* in case we are forced to start an operation with less than the normal crew size. The minimum is the smallest number of men with which it is feasible to work at all.

We will start by doing the usual CPM computations. The results are shown in Fig. 8–10.

Operation	Duration	Earliest Start	Finish	Latest Start	Finish	Float Total	Free
1–3	3	0	3	3	6	3	0
1–5	8	0	8	0	8	0	—°
1–7	4	0	4	5	9	5	0
3–9	5	3	8	6	11	3	3
5–9	3	8	11	8	11	0	—°
7–9	2	4	6	9	11	5	5

° Critical.

Fig. 8–10

Now we list the operations in order of earliest start on the scheduling work sheet, Fig. 8–11.

*Critical.

Fig. 8–11

Since this is a small project, all the operations can be considered as a single group for scheduling purposes. In Fig. 8–11 the earliest start and latest finish of each operation are indicated by brackets on the work sheet. Note that if the earliest start is computed to be day 3, the work cannot actually start until the *end* of day 3, which is the beginning of day 4 (see Chapter 7). However, if the work is scheduled for completion on a certain day, all of that day is available for work on the operation.

Let us begin by scheduling the critical operations 1–5 and 5–9. If we run out of men, we want to postpone the non-critical operations. Operation 1–5 runs from day 1 (earliest start day 0) through day 8 and requires four men. Enter a 4 in the columns for days 1 through 8 (Fig. 8–12).

Opera- tion	Dura- tion	Crew Size		Day Number																			
		Norm.	Min.	1	2	3	4	5	6	7	8	9	10	11	12	13	14	15	16	17	18	19	20
1-3	3	4	2	[				]															
1-5*	8	4	2	[4	4	4	4	4	4	4	4	4]											
1-7	4	2	1	[							]												
3-9	5	3	1				[							]									
7-9	2	5	3					[						]									
5-9*	3	2	1									[2	2	2]									
Total Required																								
Total Available																								

*Critical.

Fig. 8–12

Operation 5–9 has an earliest start on day 8. Since this means the *end* of day 8, the first full working day is day 9. This operation is completed on day 11 and requires a crew of two men. Enter a 2 in the columns for days 9, 10, and 11 for this operation. All the critical operations are now scheduled.

Turning now to the non-critical operations, we begin with operations 1–3 and 3–9, since these have the least amount of total float (3 days). Let us try to start operation 1–3 at its earliest start time, day 0 (first full working day, day 1). If we do so, we can also start operation 3–9 on day 3 (first full working day, day 4). This is shown in Fig. 8–13.

Opera- tion	Dura- tion	Crew Size		Day Number																			
		Norm.	Min.	1	2	3	4	5	6	7	8	9	10	11	12	13	14	15	16	17	18	19	20
1-3	3	4	2	[4	4	4		]															
1-5*	8	4	2	[4	4	4	4	4	4	4	4	4]											
1-7	4	2	1	[							]												
3-9	5	3	1				[3	3	3	3	3			]									
7-9	2	5	3					[						]									
5-9*	3	2	1									[2	2	2]									
Total Required																								
Total Available																								

*Critical.

Fig. 8–13

The final step is the scheduling of operations 1–7 and 7–9. Operation 1–7 is started at its early start time, but the start of

Opera-tion	Dura-tion	Crew Size		Day Number																			
		Norm.	Min.	1	2	3	4	5	6	7	8	9	10	11	12	13	14	15	16	17	18	19	20
1-3	3	4	2	[4	4	4				]													
1-5*	8	4	2	[4	4	4	4	4	4	4	4]											
1-7	4	2	1	[2	2	2	2					]											
3-9	5	3	1					[3	3	3	3	3		]									
7-9	2	5	3						[			5	5	]									
5-9*	3	2	1									[2	2	2]									
Total Required				10	10	10	9	7	7	7	7	7	7	2									
Total Available																							

*Critical.

Fig. 8–14

operation 7–9 is postponed in order to avoid a "hump" in man-power requirements in the middle of the project. The completed schedule is shown in Fig. 8–14.

The total number of men required on each day is shown on the bottom line of the work sheet in Fig. 8–14.

So far, we have made an effort to avoid peaks and fluctuations in our manpower requirements but have not considered any limitation on the number of men we may use. Suppose, now, that we have the same project as before but are restricted to a maximum of nine men on any one day. We can still complete the project in 11 days, but we must postpone some of the non-critical operations, as shown in Fig. 8–15.

Opera-tion	Dura-tion	Crew Size		Day Number																			
		Norm.	Min.	1	2	3	4	5	6	7	8	9	10	11	12	13	14	15	16	17	18	19	20
1-3	3	4	2	[4	4	4				]													
1-5*	8	4	2	[4	4	4	4	4	4	4	4]											
1-7	4	2	1	[				2	2	2	2	]											
3-9	5	3	1					[3	3	3	3	3		]									
7-9	2	5	3						[			5	5	]									
5-9*	3	2	1									[2	2	2]									
Total Required				8	8	8	9	9	9	9	7	7	7	2									
Total Available				9	9	9	9	9	9	9	9	9	9	9									

Fig. 8–15. Completed Schedule

According to the schedule of Fig. 8–15, there are several days when less than nine men are required. This suggests the possibility of a trade-off of manpower from non-critical to critical operations, as described in Chapter 7, in order to reduce the durations of the critical operations and thus speed up the overall job. Whether or not this can be done depends on the nature of the operations involved.

Suppose, for example, that the critical operation 1–5 could utilize a crew of five men with a corresponding shortening of overall duration. If we schedule this operation for 4 days with five men and 3 days with four men, we have reduced the duration by 1 day and can start the following operation 5–9 a day earlier. In order not to exceed the limit of nine men, however, we must start one of the operations at less than its normal crew size. Figure 8–16 shows operation 3–9 started with two men. (This is

Opera-tion	Dura-tion	Crew Size		Day Number																			
		Norm.	Min.	1	2	3	4	5	6	7	8	9	10	11	12	13	14	15	16	17	18	19	20
1-3	3	4	2	[4	4	4	]																
1-5*	8	4	2	[5	5	5	5	4	4	4	]												
1-7	4	2	1	[			2	2	2	2	]												
3-9	5	3	1				[2	3	3	3	2	2	]											
7-9	2	5	3								[5	5	]											
5-9*	3	2	1								[2	2	2]											
Total Required				9	9	9	9	9	9	9	9	9	9	2									
Total Available				9	9	9	9	9	9	9	9	9	9	9									

*Critical.

Fig. 8–16. Adjusted Schedule

possible because the minimum crew size for this operation was one man.) The duration of operation 3–9 must be extended to make up for the smaller crew. Operation 3–9 has been scheduled for two men for the first day, three men for the next 3 days, and two men for the last 2 days. This gives the same total effort (15 man-days) as the original schedule: 5 days with three men each day.

Note that the earliest start time for operation 7–9 was originally day 4. However, since we have delayed operation 1–7, we cannot start operation 7–9 until day 7 (first working day, day 8). The basic rule of CPM has not changed: we cannot start an operation until the operation preceding it has been completed.

Opera-tion	Dura-tion	Crew Size		Day Number																			
		Norm.	Min.	1	2	3	4	5	6	7	8	9	10	11	12	13	14	15	16	17	18	19	20
1-3	3	4	2	[2	2	2	2	4	]														
1-5*	8	4	2	[4	4	4	4	4	4	4	4	]											
1-7	4	2	1	[2	2	2	2					]											
3-9	5	3	1						[3	3	3	3	1	2]									
7-9	2	5	3						[			3	5	3]									
5-9*	3	2	1									[2	2	2]									
Total Required				8	8	8	8	8	8	7	7	7	8	8	7								
Total Available				8	8	8	8	8	8	8	8	8	8	8									

Fig. 8–17. Schedule Using Eight Men

Suppose, now, that we have only *eight* men with which to complete the project. A number of schedules are possible; one is shown in Fig. 8–17. Here operations 1–3, 3–9, and 7–9 have been "stretched out"—using a crew size smaller than the normal in order to keep the total number of men down to a maximum of eight per day. In this case no attempt was made to shorten the critical operations by trading off manpower.

A little calculation will show that the job must take at least 11 days if only eight men are available. The total effort (in man-days) can be found by multiplying the duration (days) times the crew size (men) for each day and totaling the results. This is shown below:

Operation	Duration	Normal Crew Size	Effort (man-days)
1–3	3	4	12
1–5	8	4	32
1–7	4	2	8
3–9	5	3	15
7–9	2	5	10
5–9	3	2	6
		Total	83

The total effort required to complete the job is 83 man-days. Except for variations in efficiency, this figure is independent of crew size. If the number of men working is limited to eight, there are only 80 man-days available in 10 working days; hence, the project will require at least 11 days.

Sometimes there are not enough men available to finish the project within the earliest finish time computed by the CPM technique. In this case the project will be extended, and the priority we have established—the critical activities first, then followed by non-critical activities in order of increasing float time—may not hold. In effect, what happens is that operations that were formerly non-critical are delayed—because of lack of resources—to the point where they become critical. The scheduling process is then one of trial and error to complete the project in the shortest possible time. The basic principles still hold, however; no operation can start until those that precede it have been completed.

In the example given previously, suppose the working force is limited to six men. Obviously, the project can no longer be completed in 11 days. Figure 8–18 shows one possible solution

Opera- tion	Dura- tion	Crew Size		Day Number																		
		Norm.	Min.	1	2	3	4	5	6	7	8	9	10	11	12	13	14	15	16	17	18	19	20
1-3	3	4	2	2	2	2	2	2	2														
1-5	8	4	2		4	4	4	4	4	4	4	4											
1-7	4	2	1								2	2	2	2									
3-9	5	3	1									3	3	3									
7-9	2	5	3												3	5	3						
5-9	3	2	1									1	1	3	3	1							
Total Required				6	6	6	6	6	6	6	6	6	6	6	6	6	3						
Total Available				6	6	6	6	6	6	6	6	6	6	6	6	6	6						

Fig. 8–18. Schedule Using Six Men

in which the completion time is extended to 14 days. Since the full number of men available (six) is utilized on each day except the last, no shorter schedule is possible. Note that some of the operations have been started with less than their normal crews. Note also that the starting dates of some of the later operations are affected by this "stretch-out." For example, operation 1–3 is prolonged until day 6. This means that work on operation 3–9 could not start until day 7. Similarly, operation 7–9 must wait until operation 1–7 is completed. *

In the examples given above, we have allowed ourselves to perform an operation using less than the normal crew. To make up for the reduced number of men, we have increased the duration so that the total effort (man-days) remained the same. In

*This is shown by the opening brackets. The actual starts are delayed further due to manpower limitations.

practice, it may be necessary to allow for a loss of efficiency when working with a crew that is larger or smaller than the optimum. In one sense, this is illustrated by Figs. 8–17 and 8–18. In both cases operation 7–9 was scheduled at less than a full crew. Since the minimum crew size is three men, we are forced to work as follows:

$$2 \text{ days @ 3 men} = 6 \text{ man-days}$$
$$1 \text{ day @ 5 men} = 5 \text{ man-days}$$
$$\text{Total} \quad \overline{11} \text{ man-days}$$

The original plan called for:

$$2 \text{ days @ 5 men} = 10 \text{ man-days}$$

The change in work plan has increased the total effort required for this operation by 1 man-day. This could not be avoided because a minimum crew size of three men was specified.

MULTIPLE PROJECT SCHEDULING

A firm that has made successful use of CPM for planning and scheduling individual projects will want to extend its use to dealing with a group of projects simultaneously. No new concepts are involved in preparing the arrow diagrams (planning). Each project may be planned independently of the others. However, if the projects must share the same pool of resources, the techniques of manpower scheduling that we have discussed can be applied.

When allocating manpower to the operations of a single project, we gave priority to the critical operations because to delay these meant to delay the entire job. When dealing with several unrelated projects, we still schedule critical operations first. If conflicts develop in sharing scarce resources, we must have some method of deciding which project will take precedence. One technique is to assign a priority or weighting factor to each project. This may be as simple as "first come, first served"—giving the highest priority to the oldest project. Or it may be an attempt to rank the projects in order of their importance to the firm.

A useful concept in preparing project priorities is *project float*. If the CPM computations show that a project may be completed in less than the time available (without considering resource limits), the project may be said to have float time. Projects with little or no leeway of this kind can be given a higher priority than those with considerable project . float. Thus, if projects must be delayed as a result of resource limitations, the ones with the most float time will be extended.

The scheduling process is the same as that which we have described, using either the graphical or work sheet method. Critical operations are scheduled first—in order of project priorities. Non-critical operations are handled in the same way—after the critical operations.

A common example of a multiple project situation is maintenance work, where a fixed maintenance crew must deal with a variety of projects. Small, uncomplicated maintenance projects may be scheduled as a group, using traditional bar-chart scheduling. As the projects become larger and more complex, CPM techniques become more valuable and can be combined with the bar chart to produce an overall schedule.

One particular advantage of CPM in this type of scheduling is that it may reveal unsuspected bottlenecks that make a project seem to take longer than it actually should. At the same time, the analysis may uncover resources that are needed for only a part of the job and that can be made available for other projects.

COMPUTER SCHEDULING—PRACTICAL CONSIDERATIONS

It is possible to set up an electronic computer to perform the type of scheduling described in this chapter, and there are several computer programs * available that profess to do just that. Such programs may be of use, but there are a number of practical factors that affect scheduling that are not easy to express as a formula. A few such factors, which might cause difficulties in computer scheduling, are listed below. Needless to say, these considerations are important in manual scheduling as well.

* See page 185 for a discussion of the term "computer program."

Restrictions on Crew Size

When manpower is limited, it may not be possible to assign the number of men originally planned. We have already considered this factor and used a *minimum* crew size. This is the minimum number of people necessary to do the job; if less than this number are available, it is just not feasible to start at all.

Restrictions on the size of crew cannot always be expressed simply as a minimum size. Job requirements or union regulations may require men to work in teams of two; thus, a crew of six or four may be feasible, but not a crew of five. Certain skills or resources may be so essential to the operation that it cannot proceed without them. For example, consider an excavation using a power shovel and several trucks. It may be feasible to work with fewer trucks than planned (although less efficient), but the work cannot be done without the shovel. In each case the operation must wait until the minimum crew size and the essential elements are available.

Loss of Efficiency

A reduction in the size of the crew from the planned or "normal" size may result in loss of efficiency. This may be true even though the minimum crew size is available. In such a case the effort (man-days, man-hours) estimated to be required for the operation must be increased. This situation is one that calls for the finest type of judgment, since the effect of a change in crew size will vary from operation to operation, depending on many intangible factors.

Split Operations

Once started, some operations must be worked continuously until completed. An example is pouring a monolithic section of concrete or curing the concrete after it is poured. Other jobs can be split up or done piecemeal, when men are available. Obviously, this affects the scheduling process. This is not a simple either/or situation. There are many jobs that *can* be split up, although it is undesirable to do so. On the other hand, there are other jobs that good practice calls for splitting up and using for "filler" work.

Related Operations

Frequently, operations are not related to each other in terms of the network diagram, but good judgment calls for them to be scheduled together. This would be the case where two unrelated operations use the same piece of expensive rented equipment. Obviously, every effort should be made to schedule these operations in such a way so that the rented equipment would be kept on the job for as short a time as possible.

Grouping together several jobs that must be done by one subcontractor is another example of this type of scheduling consideration. Here, while the network may not require it, there is an advantage to the subcontractor (and possibly to the general contractor) in being able to go from one operation to the next without loss of time from starting and stopping.

These are only a few of the many practical considerations that influence the scheduling process. Even if a computer is used as an aid in scheduling, the results should be checked carefully by an experienced planner to make sure that these factors have been considered so that the resulting schedule is realistic as well as efficient.

SUMMARY

Resource scheduling combines CPM with traditional scheduling techniques. The requirements may be shown by a graph of manpower versus time or by a table showing the men required each day. In either case the process is one of trial and error. Critical operations take priority, and the non-critical operations are shifted in time within their available float to achieve the schedule desired. If the resources are not sufficient to complete the project within the computed duration, completion is extended, and, in effect, non-critical operations become critical because of lack of resources.

The same techniques may be used for allocating resources to

a group of projects, once priorities have been established among them.

Computer programs are available to assist in manpower or other resource scheduling, but computer-produced schedules should be reviewed carefully because of the many intangible factors involved.

PROBLEMS

8-1. The following network (Fig. 8–19) represents a portion of a construction project. Determine the critical path and schedule each operation,

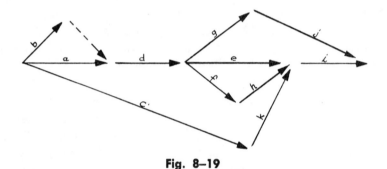

Fig. 8–19

using the graphical method. The project is to be completed in not more than 9 weeks, and ups and downs in the labor force should be as few as possible.

Operation	Duration (weeks)	Crew Size (men)
a	3	2
b	2	2
c	2	6
d	2	3
e	1	4
f	1	8
g	1	4
h	2	4
i	1	2
j	1	4
k	1	4

a) Schedule, assuming crew sizes are fixed.

b) What modifications would you make if you could vary crew size while keeping total man-weeks constant for each operation?

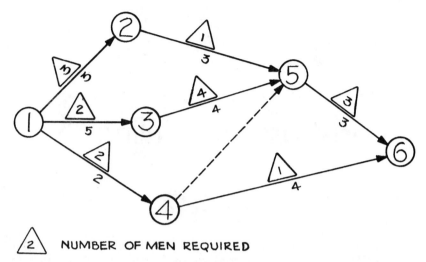

NUMBER OF MEN REQUIRED

Fig. 8–20

8–2. Refer to the network in Fig. 8–20.

    a) Schedule, using work sheet method, assuming that five men are available for this job. Do not vary crew sizes.

    b) Schedule, assuming that four men are available. Do not vary crew sizes.

    c) Schedule, assuming that four men are available. You may vary crew size if necessary, keeping total effort (man-days) constant for each operation.

9

Least-Cost Scheduling

In the previous chapters we have been mainly concerned with *time*. Now we want to introduce the second vital planning factor—*cost*. The old cliché "time is money" recognizes that there is a close relationship between these two variables. A major advantage of CPM is the ability to find a specific relation between time and cost for any project. This relation can then be used:

1. To determine the cost of speeding up, or "crashing" a project by a specified number of days.
2. To determine the most economical schedule for meeting a specified completion date.
3. To determine the *optimum schedule*—that duration that minimizes the sum of direct and indirect costs.

We will start with the relation between time and cost for a single operation and from it develop a relation for the entire project.

TIME-COST RELATIONSHIP FOR A SINGLE OPERATION

In preparing the CPM network, we have used a single estimate of time (duration) for each operation, based on a "normal" level of men, machines, and other resources. If necessary, most operations could be completed in less than the normal time. This usually requires additional resources, such as overtime, added

104

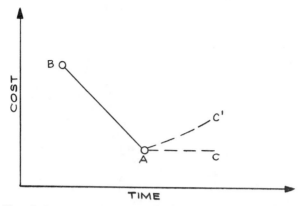

Fig. 9–1. Time-Cost Relation for a Single Operation

personnel, cost of air freight, etc. The process of shortening is known as "crashing" the operation.

In general, if we want to finish a job sooner, it usually costs more. This relationship can be represented by means of a graph of cost versus time, as shown in Fig. 9–1. Point *A* represents the cheapest (and usually the slowest) way of doing the job. This is called the *normal point*. The cost of doing the work in this way is called the *normal cost,* and the corresponding time is called the *normal duration.*

We can, of course, stretch out the operation further, as shown by the dashed line *A–C;* but since this does not lower costs, there is usually no reason to do so.* As a matter of fact, it may even increase costs, if the number of men becomes too small to work efficiently. Such an unwanted increase in cost is shown by the dashed line *A–C',* and is often called *dragout.*

As we speed up or "crash" the job, our costs go up, as shown by the line *A–B.* Finally, we reach point *B,* which is the shortest possible duration for this job. This is the *crash point.* Additional manpower or other resources would increase costs but would not shorten the job.

---

* An exception would be when making trade-offs of resources from a non-critical to a critical operation as described in Chapter 7. However, to obtain the benefit of the CPM analysis, such trade-offs should be made *after* the computations, when the critical operations are known. For the initial computations the normal duration should be assumed.

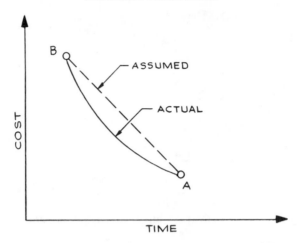

Fig. 9–2. Actual and Assumed Time-Cost Relation

A–B is called the *time-cost curve.* We have shown this curve as a straight line. Actually, it could have any shape, depending on what type of operation we are concerned with. In most cases, however, the curve can be approximated by a straight line drawn between the crash point and the normal point, as shown in Fig. 9–2.

In exceptional cases the curve can be shown by a series of straight lines as in Fig. 9–3.

There are cases where the relationship between time and cost does not result in a continuous curve. This would occur where there are only two or more distinct ways of accomplishing the

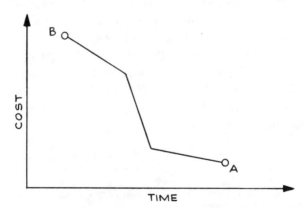

Fig. 9–3. Irregular Time-Cost Relation

operation, and no "in-between" possibilities. An example would be a material purchase for which there are two sources of supply, each offering a different delivery time. In this case the time-cost curve would consist of two points only. A graph of this type is shown in Fig. 9–4.

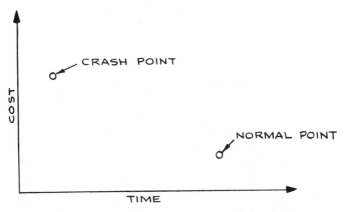

Fig. 9–4. "Either-Or" Time-Cost Relation

THE COST SLOPE

If we know the shape of the time-cost curve for a given operation, we can find out how much it would cost to shorten the operation by *1 day*. If the time-cost curve is a straight line, then the cost to shorten the operation by 1 day is the same as the slope of this line. The cost per day to shorten a job is oalled the *cost slope* and is found by the following rule:

$$\text{Cost Slope} = \frac{\text{Cost per day}}{\text{to shorten}} = \frac{\text{Crash Cost} - \text{Normal Cost}}{\text{Normal Duration} - \text{Crash Duration}}$$

For example, consider the operation with the time-cost curve shown in Fig. 9–5. The factors are as follows:

	Normal	*Crash*
Time	7	5
Cost	$800	$900

It costs $100 to shorten the operation by 2 days, and the cost slope (cost to shorten by 1 day) is $50.

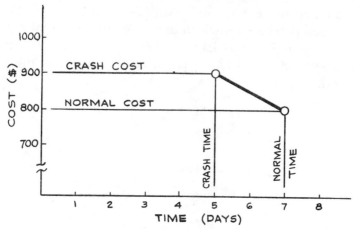

Fig. 9–5. Finding the Cost Slope

Where the time-cost curve is a series of straight lines, we must compute a separate cost slope for each segment. However, in the vast majority of cases, a single line connecting the crash point and normal point will suffice.

The cost slope is a very useful concept in shortening a project, since we can use it to compute the additional cost of shortening an operation by any amount. For example, if the cost slope is $30 per day, it will cost $90 to shorten the operation by 3 days. Of course, we cannot shorten the operation to less than its crash time.

TIME-COST RELATION FOR A PROJECT

So far, we have been concerned about the relation between time and cost for a single operation. A similar relation exists for the project as a whole. To find the time-cost curve for a complete project, we start with all operations at their normal points. If we add up the normal costs of each operation, we obtain the normal cost for the project. The duration—found by the usual CPM computations—gives the normal project duration. These factors give the normal point—first point on the time-cost curve.

We then proceed to shorten the project by shortening or "crashing" the critical operations. At each step the additional cost to shorten is found from the cost slopes of the operations being shortened. By adding these increments of cost, we find the new project cost corresponding to each new project duration. Each step in the shortening process yields a new point on the time-cost curve. The typical time-cost curve has the appearance of that shown in Fig. 9–6.

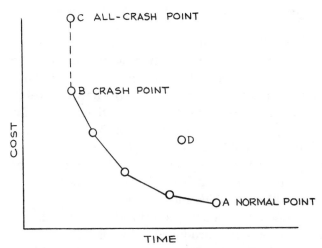

Fig. 9–6. Typical Project Time-Cost Curve

In general, the curve consists of a series of short, straight segments and is concave upward. As the shortening continues, a point is reached at which no further shortening is possible. This is the *crash point* for the project (point *B* in Fig. 9–6). At this point some of the operations have not yet reached their minimums (crash points). If these operations are shortened further, costs are increased with no saving on project time. This is shown by the vertical line *B–C*. When all operations have reached their crash points, the total project cost is at a maximum. This point, *C*, is called the *all-crash point*.

USE OF COST SLOPES TO SHORTEN A PROJECT

In Chapter 7 we learned that to shorten a project it is necessary to shorten the critical operations. Knowing the cost slopes

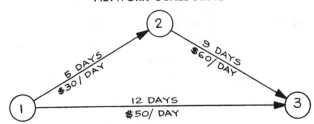

Fig. 9–7. Use of Cost Slopes for Project Shortening

of each operation permits us to shorten in the most economical manner, by crashing the operations with the lowest cost slope first. For example, consider the simple network shown in Fig. 9–7. Cost slopes for each operation are shown under the arrows.

The critical path consists of operations 1–2 and 2–3. To shorten the project, we must shorten one of these two operations. Obviously, we would choose operation 1–2 with a cost slope of $30 per day in preference to 2–3, which costs $60 per day to shorten. Only when 1–2 had reached its crash point (shortest time) would we consider shortening 2–3.

As the operations along the critical path are shortened, new critical paths may be introduced. It is then necessary to shorten along parallel critical paths. In the network of Fig. 9–7, once operations 1–2 and 2–3 have been shortened so that their combined time is 12 days, operation 1–3 becomes critical. If the project is to be shortened further, both paths must be reduced.

At no time during the shortening process should we crash any non-critical operation, since to do so increases costs without reducing project time. Similarly, it is essential to select operations to be shortened in proper sequence—as determined by the cost slopes. Either error will cause the points determined to lie above the minimum curve A–B (Fig. 9–6) at some higher cost, say D.

DIRECT AND INDIRECT COSTS

The costs that are directly related to the individual operations are known as *direct costs*. These include labor, materials, and transportation. The time-cost curve we have been talking about shows these direct costs. Other costs associated with the project as a whole, but not dependent on individual operations, are known as *indirect costs*. Common examples of indirect costs are:

1. Wages of project supervisor and other non-hourly personnel
2. Rent and utilities costs for a field office
3. Clerical costs
4. Interest on borrowed funds
5. Rental of office equipment, trucks, etc.

In general, although indirect costs cannot be associated specifically with any one operation, they tend to increase with time. Some contracts specify penalty and bonus clauses; that is, there is a bonus for early completion and a penalty for late completion. Obviously, these costs are also related to time and can be considered part of the indirect project costs.

To determine the total cost of a project, it is necessary to estimate the indirect costs. This can often be done from accounting records, or from knowledge of the supervisory and other related costs that apply to the job.

TOTAL PROJECT COST

The total cost for a project is the sum of the direct and the indirect costs. Since both of these costs vary with time, it is convenient to show both costs on a single time-cost graph. The total project cost at any duration will be the sum of the two curves at that point. By adding in this way, a curve of *total* job cost can be obtained, as shown in Fig. 9–8.

Study of the curve of total job cost shows that the cost is a minimum at a certain duration. This point is the *optimum duration,* which is that schedule that yields the lowest combination of direct and indirect costs. If contractual and other conditions permit, this is the duration at which the project should be scheduled, since the associated total cost is at a minimum.

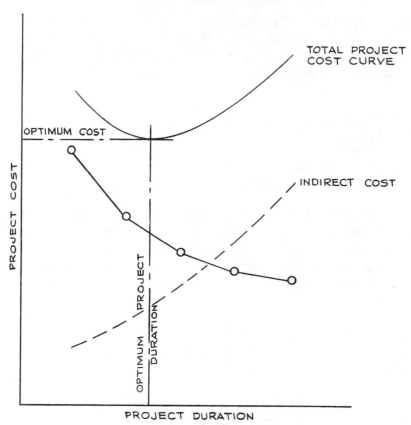

Fig. 9–8. Typical Total Project Cost Curve

ILLUSTRATION OF LEAST-COST SCHEDULING

Now that we have covered the principles of least-cost scheduling, let us see how they are applied to a simple network. We will use additional work sheets * to keep track of the shortening and to help in finding the operations with the lowest cost slopes. For our example, consider the simple network shown in Fig. 9–9.

---

* Some of the work sheets used in this chapter were suggested in part by forms in John W. Fondahl, *A Non-Computer Approach to the Critical Path Method for the Construction Industry* (2d ed.; Stanford: Stanford University, Department of Civil Engineering, 1962).

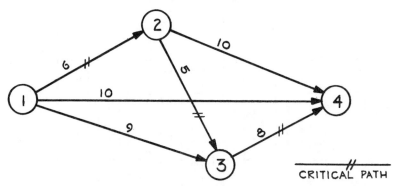

Fig. 9–9. Initial Network—All Operations at Normal Times

The estimated times, together with corresponding costs, are tabulated in columns 3 through 6 of Work Sheet No. 1, shown in Fig. 9–10. The total cost to shorten (crash) each operation to its shortest duration (crash point) is found by subtracting the normal cost (column 4) from the crash cost (column 3). This is entered in column 7. To find the total number of days by which the operation can be shortened, subtract the crash time (column 6) from the normal time (column 5), and enter the result in column 8. Finally, find the cost slope by dividing the figure in column 7 by that in column 8, and enter the result in column 9. These preliminary computations are shown in Fig. 9–10.

To find the normal cost of the entire project, simply add up the individual normal costs shown in column 4. This is found to be $1,300. The normal duration is found by the "forward pass" of the usual CPM computations, using the normal times. Scanning the diagram, the normal duration is found to be 19 days.

A duration of 19 days at a cost of $1,300 is the first point on the time-cost curve for the project. Enter the total duration of 19 days on line (*a*) (Project Duration) at the bottom of Work Sheet No. 1 under Cycle 0, and the total project cost on line (*e*) (New Project Cost). The "cycles" referred to here are the successive steps by which the project is shortened. The first cycle involves no shortening and for that reason is designated 0 rather

Operation		Cost ($)		Duration (days)		Cost Increment (3)-(4)	Maximum Days Shortening (5)-(6)	Cost per Day To Shorten (7) ÷ (8) $/Day	Cycle						
											Days Shortened				
i	j	Crash	Normal	Normal	Crash				0	1	2	3	4	5	6
(1)	(2)	(3)	(4)	(5)	(6)	(7)	(8)	(9)							
1	2	160	100	6	5	60	1	60							
1	3	360	200	9	5	160	4	40							
1	4	500	400	10	6	100	4	25							
2	3	120	60	5	3	60	2	30							
2	4	650	300	10	5	350	5	70							
3	4	360	240	8	6	120	2	60							
Total			1,300												

a) Project Duration
b) Total Number of Days Reduced
c) Total Cost per Day To Shorten
d) Increase in Cost
e) New Project Cost

Fig. 9–10. Work Sheet No. 1—Preliminary

than 1. Since no operation has been shortened, there are no other entries in the Cycle 0 column.

To start the shortening process, we recall that we must reduce the activities along the critical path. The activity we will choose will be the one with the least cost slope, since this will produce the desired shortening at lowest cost.

The critical operations are 1–2, 2–3, and 3–4. From column 9 of Work Sheet No. 1, operation 2–3 has the lowest cost slope of the three: $30 per day. Column 8 indicates that this operation can be shortened by 2 days. However, we must check to make sure that we do not introduce any new critical paths. Let us attempt to shorten operation 2–3 by 2 days. Enter "2" under Cycle 1 in the "Days Shortened" column of Work Sheet No. 1 in line with operation 2–3. A check of the diagram shows that shortening operation 2–3 by 2 days does actually shorten the project by this same amount. Now we may enter a "2" on line (b) (Total Number of Days Reduced) of Work Sheet No. 1 under Cycle 1. (See Fig. 9–11.) The new project duration (17 days) is found directly from the CPM computations. Enter 17 on line (a) under Cycle 1.

The total cost per day to shorten the project is simply the cost of shortening operation 2–3, which is $30 per day. Enter this on line (c) (Total Cost per Day To Shorten) of Work Sheet No. 1. The overall increase in project cost is found by multiplying line (b) by line (c):

$$2 \times \$30 = \$60$$

The result is entered on line (d) (Increase in Cost). Line (d) is then added to the previous project cost, line (e), Cycle 0, to find the new project cost of $1,360. This is entered on line (e) under Cycle 1. An alternate way of computing the new project cost, which may be used as a check, is to sum up the individual operation costs.

We have now completed the first shortening cycle, which yields a second point on the time-cost curve: a duration of 17 days at a cost of $1,360. Work Sheet No. 1 now appears as shown in Fig. 9–11. Figure 9–12 shows the first two points on the time-

Operation		Cost ($)		Duration (days)		Cost Increment (3)-(4)	Maximum Days Shortening (5)-(6)	Cost per Day To Shorten (7)÷(8) $/Day	Cycle Days Shortened						
i	j	Crash	Normal	Normal	Crash				0	1	2	3	4	5	6
(1)	(2)	(3)	(4)	(5)	(6)	(7)	(8)	(9)							
1	2	160	100	6	5	60	1	60							
1	3	360	200	9	5	160	4	40							
1	4	500	400	10	6	100	4	25							
2	3	120	60	5	3	60	2	30		2					
2	4	650	300	10	5	350	5	70							
3	4	360	240	8	6	120	2	60							
Total			1,300												

a) Project Duration — 19 | 17
b) Total Number of Days Reduced — 2
c) Total Cost per Day To Shorten — 30
d) Increase in Cost — 60
e) New Project Cost — 1,300 | 1,360

Fig. 9–11. Work Sheet No. 1 After First Shortening Cycle

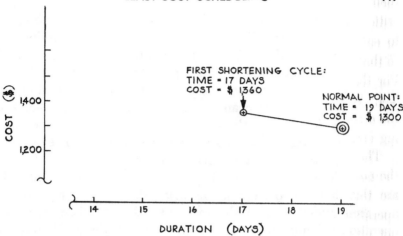

Fig. 9–12. Time-Cost Curve After First Shortening Cycle

cost curve: the normal point (least cost) and the point found by the first shortening cycle. These points are connected by a straight line to give the first piece of the time-cost curve.

In this first shortening cycle there was only one critical path, and it was quite easy to decide which operation should be shortened. However, when there is more than one critical path, the process is facilitated by the use of Work Sheet No. 2 shown in Fig. 9–13.

Operation		Critical Paths	Cost Slope $/Day	Cost To Shorten Cycle					
i	j			1					
1	2	x	60						
1	3		40						
1	4		25						
2	3	⊗	30	30					
2	4		70						
3	4	x	60						
		Total		30					

Fig. 9–13. Least-Cost Scheduling—Work Sheet No. 2, Cycle 1

To use Work Sheet No. 2, fill in the operation numbers and their cost slopes from Work Sheet No. 1. After identifying the critical path from the basic CPM computations, make an X next to each critical operation in the space labeled "Critical Paths" so that each critical path is identified by a vertical column of X's. For the first cycle place an X next to operations 1–2, 2–3, and 3–4. When looking for the operation with least cost slope, only the operations marked with X's need be examined. The remaining (non-critical) operations may be ignored.

The columns labeled "Cost To Shorten" are used to tabulate the cost slopes of the operations being shortened. These slopes are then added to find the total cost slope. When only one operation is being shortened (as in Cycle 1), these columns are not necessary, but they are useful when several operations are being shortened, as we shall see.

Before going on to the second cycle, note that we have entered a "2" under Cycle 1 for operation 2–3 on Work Sheet No. 1 (Fig. 9–11). This indicates that operation 2–3 was shortened by 2 days in the first cycle. Comparing this to column 8, we note that we have used up all the available shortening on this operation. (It has reached its crash point.) To show that operation 2–3 is now out of consideration for future shortening, circle the X next to operation 2–3 on Work Sheet No. 2 (Fig. 9–13).

To proceed with Cycle 2, we first revise the network diagram to show the new operation times, as shown in Fig. 9–14.

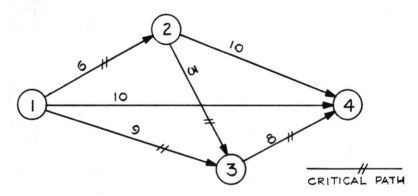

Fig. 9–14. Network After Completion of First Shortening Cycle

The CPM computations show that we now have two parallel critical paths:

a) 1–2, 2–3, and 3–4
b) 1–3 and 3–4

We have already marked the first path on Work Sheet No. 2. Now add a second column of X's to show the new path (Fig. 9–15).

Operation		Critical Paths	Cost Slope $/Day	Cost To Shorten Cycle					
i	j			1	2				
1	2	x	60						
1	3	x	40						
1	4		25						
2	3	⊗	30	30					
2	4		70						
3	4	x x	60		60				
		Total		30	60				

Fig. 9–15. Work Sheet No. 2 for Second Cycle

If we want to shorten the project, we must shorten both paths at once. Work Sheet No. 2 is used to select the combination of operations having the lowest total of cost slopes. Operation 3–4 (cost slope $60 per day) is common to both critical paths. By shortening it, we can satisfy the requirement of shortening along both paths. The only other possibility is the combination of operations 1–2 and 1–3, with a total cost slope of $60 + $40 = $100. Operation 3–4 is the logical choice. Enter its slope under Cycle 2 on Work Sheet No. 2 (Fig. 9–15).

Since only one operation is being shortened, the total cost slope is also $60. This is carried forward to Work Sheet No. 1, line (*c*), under Cycle 2 (Fig. 9–16). Column 8 of Work Sheet No. 1 tells us that the maximum shortening possible for operation 3–4 is 2 days. However, if we reduce operation 3–4 by 2 days

Operation		Cost ($)		Duration (days)		Cost Increment (3)-(4)	Maximum Days Shortening (5)-(6)	Cost per Day To Shorten (7)÷(8) $/Day	Cycle						
i	j	Crash	Normal	Normal	Crash				0	1	2	3	4	5	6
(1)	(2)	(3)	(4)	(5)	(6)	(7)	(8)	(9)			Days Shortened				
1	2	160	100	6	5	60	1	60							
1	3	360	200	9	5	160	4	40							
1	4	500	400	10	6	100	4	25							
2	3	120	60	5	3	60	2	30		2					
2	4	650	300	10	5	350	5	70							
3	4	360	240	8	6	120	2	60			1				
Total			1,300												

a) Project Duration   19   17   16
b) Total Number of Days Reduced   2   1
c) Total Cost per Day To Shorten   30   60
d) Increase in Cost   60   60
e) New Project Cost   1,300   1,360   1,420

Fig. 9-16. Work Sheet No. 1 After Second Cycle

and perform the CPM computations, we find that the project has been shortened by only 1 day. Apparently, a new critical path has been introduced. Hence, we must limit our shortening on Cycle 2 to 1 day.

To see why this is so, recall that we want to shorten the project at the least possible cost. Shortening operation 3–4 by 2 days costs $120, but gains only 1 day in terms of project completion. Shortening operation 3–4 by a single day has the same effect on the project, but at half the cost.

Enter a shortening of 1 day next to operation 3–4 on Work Sheet No. 1 under Cycle 2. Enter the new project duration on line (a) (16 days) and the total amount by which the project is shortened (1 day) on line (b). The cost per day to shorten is taken from Work Sheet No. 2 ($60) and is entered on line (c). Compute the total increase in cost by multiplying line (b) times line (c) and enter the increase ($60) on line (d). As in Cycle 1, add this to the previous project cost to find the new project cost ($1,420). This step completes Cycle 2 and yields another point on the time-cost curve: a duration of 16 days at a cost of $1,420.

Before erasing any of the figures on our network in preparation for the next shortening cycle, it might be well to enter the various durations we have obtained at each cycle on Work Sheet No. 3 shown in Fig. 9–17. This work sheet will be used later

SCHEDULE SUMMARIES

Operation \ Project Duration	Durations						
	19	17	16				
1-2	6	6	6				
1-3	9	9	9				
1-4	10	10	10				
2-3	5	3	3				
2-4	10	10	10				
3-4	8	8	7				

Fig. 9–17. Work Sheet No. 3 After Second Cycle

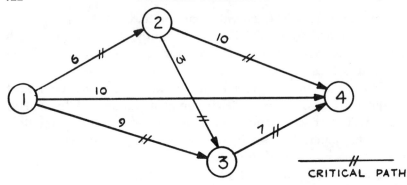

Fig. 9–18. Network After Completion of Second Shortening Cycle

when we have selected one particular project duration. It will show us just how to schedule each operation in order to achieve the desired duration at the least possible cost.

The network for Cycle 3 appears as shown in Fig. 9–18. There are now three parallel critical paths:

    a) 1–2 and 2–4
    b) 1–2, 2–3, and 3–4
    c) 1–3 and 3–4

We have already marked two of these paths on Work Sheet No. 2. Now add an additional column of X's to identify the new path (Fig. 9–19).

Operation		Critical Paths	Cost Slope $/Day	Cost To Shorten Cycle					
i	j			1	2	3			
1	2	x x	60			60			
1	3	x	40						
1	4		25						
2	3	⊗	30	30	(–)30				
2	4	x	70						
3	4	x x	60		60	60			
		Total		30	60	90			

Fig. 9–19. Work Sheet No. 2 for Third Cycle

To shorten the project, we must shorten *all three* paths at once. Our object is now to select the combination of operations having the smallest total of cost slopes. From Work Sheet No. 2 we have the following combinations of operations (taking advantage of the fact that some operations are common to more than one path):

Operation		Cost Slope
a) 1–2		$ 60
1–3		40
	Total	$100
b) 1–2		$ 60
3–4		60
	Total	$120
c) 2–4		$ 70
3–4		60
	Total	$130

It would appear that the least expensive combination of operations is 1–2 plus 1–3, at a total cost of $100 per day. In this case, however, there is a cheaper way to shorten. If we simultaneously shorten operations 1–2 and 3–4, at a total cost of $120, we find that we introduce *float time* into operation 2–3, an operation that was previously shortened. (Check the network of Fig. 9–18 to verify this.) We can take advantage of this float by stretching out operation 2–3 by 1 day with a *savings* of $30. Tabulating the plus and minus cost slopes of these operations under Cycle 2 on Work Sheet No. 2 (Fig. 9–19), we find the net cost per day to be $90.

Returning to Work Sheet No. 1, we find that operations 1–2 and 3–4 can each be shortened by only 1 day. Enter a shortening of 1 day next to operations 1–2 and 3–4 on Work Sheet No. 1 (Cycle 2) and a *lengthening* of 1 day next to operation 2–3. (This may be shown by a plus sign; all other quantities are understood to be minus). Enter the new project duration (15 days), the days reduced (1), and the total cost per day to shorten ($90); and compute the total increase in cost (1 × $90 = $90). As in previous cycles, add this increase to the total project cost of the preceding cycle to find the new project cost of $1,510.

Work Sheet No. 1 now appears as in Fig. 9–20. We have now completed Cycle 3 and have obtained another point on the time-cost curve: a duration of 15 days at a cost of $1,510.

Operation		Cost ($)		Duration (days)		Cost Increment (3)-(4)	Maximum Days Shortening (5)-(6)	Cost per Day To Shorten (7)÷(8) $/Day	Cycle						
i	j	Crash	Normal	Normal	Crash				0	1	2	3	4	5	6
(1)	(2)	(3)	(4)	(5)	(6)	(7)	(8)	(9)							
											Days Shortened				
1	2	160	100	6	5	60	1	60							
1	3	360	200	9	5	160	4	40				1			
1	4	500	400	10	6	100	4	25							
2	3	120	60	5	3	60	2	30		2		+1			
2	4	650	300	10	5	350	5	70							
3	4	360	240	8	6	120	2	60			1	1			
Total			1,300												

a) Project Duration | 19 | 17 | 16 | 15
b) Total Number of Days Reduced | | 2 | 1 | 1
c) Total Cost per Day To Shorten | | 30 | 60 | 90
d) Increase in Cost | | 60 | 60 | 90
e) New Project Cost | 1,300 | 1,360 | 1,420 | 1,510

Fig. 9–20. Work Sheet No. 1 After Third Cycle

SCHEDULE SUMMARIES

Operation	Project Duration	Durations						
		19	17	16	15			
1-2		6	6	6	5			
1-3		9	9	9	9			
1-4		10	10	10	10			
2-3		5	3	3	4			
2-4		10	10	10	10			
3-4		8	8	7	6			

Fig. 9–21. Work Sheet No. 3 After Third Cycle

Before proceeding to the fourth cycle, we enter the operation durations on Work Sheet No. 3 (Fig. 9–21).

The network for Cycle 4 appears as shown in Fig. 9–22. The critical paths remain as before. We have used up all the shortening possible on both operations 1–2 and 3–4, so we circle the

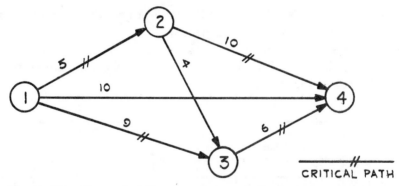

Fig. 9–22. Network After Completion of Third Shortening Cycle

X's next to these operations. However, operation 2–3 has been expanded by 1 day and is once again available for shortening. To show this, erase the circle around the X next to this operation (Fig. 9–23).

From Work Sheet No. 2 there is only one combination of operations left that will include an operation from each of the three critical paths. This is 1–3, 2–3, and 2–4. Shortening is limited by that available for operation 2–3 (1 day). Using Work Sheet No. 2, we find the total cost for this combination to be $140 per day. Entering this cost and the 1-day shortening time

| Operation | | Critical Paths | Cost Slope $/Day | Cost To Shorten Cycle | | | | | | |
i	j			1	2	3	4			
1	2	⊗ ⊗	60			60				
1	3	x	40				40			
1	4		25							
2	3	x	30	30		(−)30	30			
2	4	x	70				70			
3	4	⊗ ⊗	60		60	60				
		Total		30	60	90	140			

Fig. 9–23. Work Sheet No. 2 for Fourth Cycle

on Work Sheet No. 1, we find the new project duration and cost to be 14 days and $1,650, respectively.

The final appearance of Work Sheet No. 2 (after the fourth cycle) is shown in Fig. 9–24. Work Sheet No. 1 is shown in its· final form in Fig. 9–25.

| Operation | | Critical Paths | Cost Slope $/Day | Cost To Shorten Cycle | | | | | | |
i	j			1	2	3	4			
1	2	⊗ ⊗	60			60				
1	3	x	40				40			
1	4		25							
2	3	⊗	30	30		(−)30	30			
2	4	x	70				70			
3	4	⊗ ⊗	60		60	60				
		Total		30	60	90	140			

Fig. 9–24. Work Sheet No. 2 After Fourth Cycle

Operation		Cost ($)		Duration (days)		Cost Increment (3)-(4)	Maximum Days Shortening (5)-(6)	Cost per Day To Shorten (7)÷(8) $/Day	Cycle						
		Crash	Normal	Normal	Crash						Days Shortened				
i	j	(3)	(4)	(5)	(6)	(7)	(8)	(9)	0	1	2	3	4	5	6
(1)	(2)														
1	2	160	100	6	5	60	1	60							
1	3	360	200	9	5	160	4	40				1	1		
1	4	500	400	10	6	100	4	25							
2	3	120	60	5	3	60	2	30		2		+1	1		
2	4	650	300	10	5	350	5	70							
3	4	360	240	8	6	120	2	60			1	1	1		
Total			1,300												
a) Project Duration									19	17	16	15	14		
b) Total Number of Days Reduced										2	1	1	1		
c) Total Cost per Day To Shorten										30	60	90	140		
d) Increase in Cost										60	60	90	140		
e) New Project Cost									1,300	1,360	1,420	1,510	1,650		

Fig. 9–25. Work Sheet No. 1 After Fourth Cycle

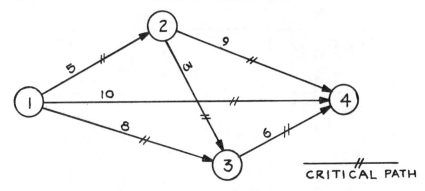

Fig. 9–26. Final Network After Completion of Fourth Cycle

Look at the network in Fig. 9–26. Several operations have not yet reached their crash time, and operation 1–4 has not been shortened at all. However, shortening these operations will not reduce the project time. This means that we have now reached the shortest possible project time—the *crash time*—and have found the complete time-cost curve for direct costs. Figure 9–27 shows this curve.

Throughout the crashing process, we have shortened only

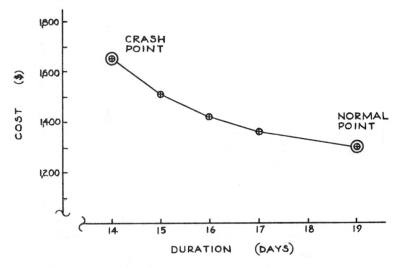

Fig. 9–27. Completed Time-Cost Curve for Direct Costs

SCHEDULE SUMMARIES

Operation	Project Duration	Durations					
		19	17	16	15	14	
1-2		6	6	6	5	5	
1-3		9	9	9	9	8	
1-4		10	10	10	10	10	
2-3		5	3	3	4	3	
2-4		10	10	10	10	9	
3-4		8	8	7	6	6	

Fig. 9–28. Work Sheet No. 3—Final Form

critical operations, and each time we chose the operations with the lowest combination of cost slopes. This means that the curve of Fig. 9–27 represents the most economical way to complete the project within any given duration from 14 to 19 days. Figure 9–28 shows the details of the schedules represented by each point on the time-cost curve.

SAMPLE PROBLEM—INDIRECT AND TOTAL COSTS

With the direct costs known, we now turn to the indirect costs. As previously stated, these are costs that are associated with the project as a whole, but not with any one operation. For this problem let us assume that the indirect costs are $400, if the project lasts 14 days. For each day the project is extended beyond 14 days, indirect costs increase by $70 per day.

At any given duration the total project cost will be the sum of the direct and indirect costs. The direct costs (taken either from the curve of Fig. 9–27 or from Work Sheet No. 1), the indirect costs, and the total costs are tabulated as follows:

Duration (days)	Direct Cost ($)	Indirect Cost ($)	Total Cost ($)
19	1,300	750	2,050
17	1,360	610	1,970
16	1,420	540	1,960
15	1,510	470	1,980
14	1,650	400	2,050

SAMPLE PROBLEM—OPTIMUM DURATION

The graph in Fig. 9–29 shows the direct cost, indirect cost, and total cost for each possible project duration. The total cost is at a minimum at a duration of 16 days. This is the optimum time (duration) for the project. The schedule that will yield this du-

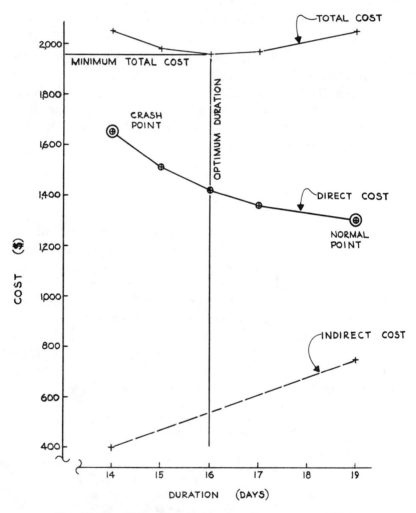

Fig. 9–29. Time-Cost Curve for Illustrative Problem

ration most economically is found from Work Sheet No. 3 (Fig. 9–28) under a duration of 16. If the optimum completion time cannot be used because of contractual commitments or for other reasons, the total cost curve can be used to show the cost of any alternate schedule, or the "penalty" for deviating from the optimum. Given a desired project duration, from 14 to 19 days, Work Sheet No. 3 will show the most economical schedule to achieve that duration.

SUMMARY OF PROCEDURE

The step-by-step procedure in shortening a project, which we have just illustrated, can be summarized as follows:

1. Draw the arrow diagram in the usual manner.
2. Instead of a single estimate of duration, prepare two time estimates as follows:
   a) The normal duration: the time it would take to do the operation in the least expensive manner.
   b) The crash duration: the shortest time in which the operation could possibly be finished, regardless of cost.
3. Estimate the *cost* of each of these alternatives.
4. Compute and tabulate the cost slope of each operation from the following formula:

$$\text{Cost Slope} = \frac{\text{Crash Cost} - \text{Normal Cost}}{\text{Normal Duration} - \text{Crash Duration}}$$

5. Perform the CPM computations, using the normal durations to determine the normal project duration.
6. Add up the normal costs of all the operations to determine the normal cost of the project. These factors determine the *normal point* on the project time-cost curve.
7. To find the shape of the project cost curve, shorten the critical operations, one by one, beginning with the operation(s) having the lowest cost slope(s). Each operation is shortened until either:
   a) Its crash time is reached, or
   b) A new critical path is formed.
8. When a new critical path is formed, shorten the combination of operations having the lowest *combined* cost slope. Where

several parallel paths exist, it is necessary to shorten simultaneously along each of them if the overall project time is to be reduced.

9. At each step, check to see if float time has been introduced in any of the operations previously shortened. If so, perhaps these operations can be *expanded* to reduce costs.

10. At each shortening cycle, compute the new project cost and duration. Plot these points on a time-cost graph.

11. Continue until no further shortening is possible. This is the *crash point*.

12. Compute the indirect project costs and plot them on the same time-cost graph.

13. Add the direct and indirect costs to find the total project cost at each duration.

14. Use the total cost curve to find the optimum time (completion at lowest cost) or the cost of any other desired schedule.

MEANING OF DIRECT AND INDIRECT COSTS

A further word is in order on the subject of direct and indirect costs. These terms are often used by accountants with meanings somewhat different from those we have used here. As a matter of fact, the exact difference between direct and indirect costs will vary from firm to firm, depending on the nature of the business and the accounting techniques in use.

As used in this text, *direct costs* refer to those costs that can be directly related to the individual operation. Generally, direct costs increase as the operation is shortened. For example, direct labor is a direct cost.

By *indirect costs* we mean those *project* costs that cannot be associated with an individual operation, but are affected by the duration of the project. For example, for our purposes rental of a field office is an indirect cost, but main office overhead is not. Some companies treat payroll taxes and fringe benefits as an indirect expense. In least-cost scheduling, we must consider these as *direct* costs, since they vary directly with the number of man-hours spent on the operation.

Some companies apply a percentage to the cost of each project to cover overhead and general administrative expenses. This is a convenient accounting device for dividing these costs among the year's jobs, but since these general administrative costs are not affected by the project duration, they are not true "costs" of the project. Hence, they are not "indirect costs" as we have defined them and should be excluded.

There are other types of indirect costs that may not show up on the books of account, but should be considered in a least-cost scheduling analysis. One such cost is lost income. To the owner of a building under construction, this can be a significant and important factor, either because of the rental income he is losing, or because of the cost of providing alternate space for his own use while waiting for the building to be completed.

A contractor is also concerned with lost income. If he is to be paid upon completion, the longer the job takes, the longer he must wait for payment. If he has borrowed money to finance the work, the longer the project takes, the more interest he must pay. Interest is an obvious out-of-pocket cost, but even if he finances the work himself, he is losing interest on his money while waiting for payment. This type of indirect cost is directly related to project duration and should be included in the analysis.

APPLICATIONS OF LEAST-COST SCHEDULING

The process of determining the true minimum cost-time curves for direct, indirect, and total project costs is called *least-cost scheduling*. It is potentially the most powerful and far-reaching use for CPM yet developed.

Least-cost scheduling can be used to find the optimum time in which to complete a project—the time for which the total of direct and indirect costs is a minimum. There are many reasons why it is not always possible to select this duration. If the project is a contract, the contractor is usually governed by a fixed completion date. In other types of projects, commitments may already have been made that make adherence to the optimum schedule impossible.

The curves can be used to determine the cost of any other completion schedule. Equally important is the fact that once a completion date has been selected, the least-cost computations will reveal the most economical way to meet this schedule.

At the beginning of this chapter, we alluded to the possibility of trading off time for money, or money for time. The completed curves make it possible to determine just how much costs would be increased by a proposed shift in the project's completion date. With this kind of information, owners can establish more realistic completion dates for projects.

HOW PRACTICAL IS LEAST-COST SCHEDULING?

Although the procedure for crashing a project is not difficult, it becomes complicated if applied to a network of any great size. Computational routines (known as *algorithms*) have been developed to handle a network of any size. Some of these routines are suitable for manual computations. Use of these techniques is taken up in advanced CPM studies.

A number of computer programs have also been developed to accomplish the crashing process. All these programs have certain limitations, however. For one thing, since the location of the critical path is not known in advance, it is necessary to prepare two time and cost estimates for each operation; when the computations are done manually, the extra estimates need be prepared only for the operations that are critical or become critical. In a large network this is a substantial saving in planning and estimating.

A more fundamental limitation of computer methods for crashing a project is the fact that the machine can crash only mechanically, in accordance with the cost slopes. In practice, however, as a project is shortened, it is often necessary to revise some of the time estimates, and even some of the network relationships. For example, changing the method of accomplishment for one operation may require a change in the method of accomplishing some other operation. Adjustments of this type require human judgment and are facilitated by manual computations. Other limitations of machine methods are discussed in Chapters 13 and 14.

SOME USEFUL APPROXIMATIONS

Even if least-cost scheduling methods are not used in their entirety to obtain the complete time-cost curve, an understanding of the principles can be valuable in shortening a project or in making other types of scheduling adjustments. Basically, the principles are:

1. Shorten only critical operations.
2. Select the operation(s) with the lowest cost slopes.
3. If there is more than one critical path, shorten simultaneously along each path.

In cases where time does not permit making actual estimates of crash time and cost, useful results may still be obtained by estimating the cost slopes directly. Even if these figures are not exact, they will produce a meaningful cost curve so long as they are *relatively* correct, that is, so long as the ratio of one cost slope to another is reasonably correct.

Our rule in shortening was always to choose the operations with the lowest cost slopes. Operations with very high cost slopes may never be shortened. Thus, it may be sufficient to know that an operation has a very high cost slope, even if its numerical value is not known.

SUMMARY

Least-cost scheduling is a systematic procedure for shortening a project in the most economical way. It makes use of the concept that most operations can be done in a slower economical manner (normal time and cost) or can be speeded up to some minimum crash time, at increased cost. For each operation the cost slope is defined as the cost per day to shorten the operation, and is found from:

$$\text{Cost Slope} = \frac{\text{Crash Cost} - \text{Normal Cost}}{\text{Normal Time} - \text{Crash Time}}$$

The curve of direct cost versus completion time (time-cost curve) for the project is found by shortening (crashing) the critical operations, beginning with those having the lowest cost slopes. While the direct costs tend to decrease as the project time is extended, there are also indirect costs that tend to increase with the project length. Total cost, which is the sum of direct and indirect costs, is at a minimum at some intermediate point, the *optimum duration.*

The time-cost curves can be used to select the optimum duration, or to determine the effect on cost of any other chosen project duration.

PROBLEMS

9–1. A crew of two men is assigned to the job of excavating a hole for a footing. The work would take 4 hours for the two men. If a third man is assigned, the time could be cut down to 3 hours. Any more men would not shorten the operation; they would just get in the way. Assume that the cost of labor is $5 per hour for each man, including all fringe benefits and payroll taxes.

   a) What is the normal cost for this operation?
   b) What is the normal duration?
   c) What is the crash cost?
   d) What is the crash duration?
   e) What is the cost slope?

9–2. The network shown in Fig. 9–30 represents a highly simplified version of a construction project. In addition to the direct costs tabulated, there are certain other indirect costs to be considered. These indirect costs

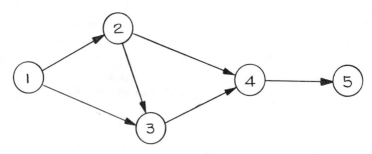

Fig. 9–30

are estimated at a flat $600 if the job lasts for 1 month or less, and will approximate $50 per working day for every day the job extends beyond a month. (Assume that a month consists of 23 working days.)

Operation	Duration (days)		Cost ($)	
	Normal	Crash	Normal	Crash
1–2	20	17	600	720
1–3	25	25	200	200
2–3	10	8	300	440
2–4	12	6	400	700
3–4	5	2	300	420
4–5	10	5	300	600

a) What is the normal cost and duration for this job?

b) Using the information given, "crash" or shorten the job step by step, using the most economical jobs, until the shortest duration (crash point) is reached.

c) At what point is a new critical path introduced?

d) Plot a graph of cost versus duration showing normal and crash points.

e) On the same graph plot a graph of total project cost. What is the minimum total project cost? What is the associated duration?

f) To achieve minimum total job cost, at what duration should each operation be scheduled?

10

PERT

PERT: A TECHNIQUE FOR DEALING WITH UNCERTAINTY

In all our work thus far, we have assumed the duration of an operation with some degree of certainty. This is usually the case with construction, manufacturing, and other types of projects where a background of experience is available. In research and development work, however, it is often impossible to give realistic time estimates for many operations. This is the case in development or design of totally new items. In construction work, a similar situation occurs when work is subject to unusual delays due to weather (for example, when working over water) or when using new and untried methods.

PERT (Program Evaluation and Review Technique) is a planning method designed to deal with this type of project. PERT starts with the same arrow diagram as CPM, but uses three time estimates to approximate the time for each operation. It also applies rules of probability to find the chances of completing a project (or part of a project) by any given date.

DEVELOPMENT OF PERT

PERT was developed by the Special Projects Office of the U. S. Navy Bureau of Ordnance, together with the management consulting firm of Booz-Allen and Hamilton, for managing the Polaris Missile program. This was an unbelievably complex project, involving research, development, design, and manufacture of totally new systems and devices. The Navy was faced with the problem of coordinating some 3,000 contractors, subcontractors, and suppliers. Through the use of PERT the Navy claims to have shaved as much as two years off the scheduled delivery date for the Polaris weapons system.

ARROW DIAGRAMMING

Like CPM, PERT uses an *arrow diagram* to represent the project. The arrows represent individual jobs or operations (which are called *activities* in PERT language). Each point where arrows meet represents an event: an instant in time marking the start or completion of one or more activities. Since PERT was originally developed for control of complex projects, management was more interested in checking up on the *events*: completion of a certain design, delivery of a piece of "hardware," etc. PERT networks usually labeled the events, rather than the activities. Other than this, the rules for drawing and numbering PERT networks are the same as those for CPM. Dummies are used when required to show proper relationships.

A network that emphasizes events is said to be *event-oriented,* and one that concentrates on the activities between events is said to be *activity-oriented.* The difference may be shown as in Fig. 10–1.

Originally, PERT networks were entirely *event-oriented* and CPM networks *activity-oriented.* Today, activity-oriented PERT is in common use so that this is no longer a real distinction be-

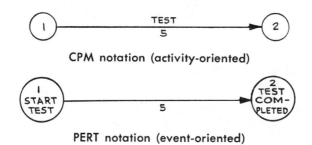

CPM notation (activity-oriented)

PERT notation (event-oriented)

Fig. 10–1. Activity-Oriented and Event-Oriented Notation

tween the two methods. We shall, however, work with event-oriented PERT in this chapter in order to provide familiarity with this type of network.

TIME ESTIMATES

The major difference between PERT and CPM comes in the step of estimating times. PERT is used for projects where there is a great deal of uncertainty about how long any given activity will take. In most cases, even the most experienced manager can give only an educated guess and his guess is subject to a wide margin of error. For this reason, the manager in charge of each activity is asked to give *three* guesses as to the time that the activity might take:

$$a = the\ optimistic\ time$$
$$b = the\ pessimistic\ time$$
$$m = the\ most\ likely\ time$$

Optimistic Time

This is the shortest possible time in which the activity could possibly be completed, assuming that everything goes well. There is only one chance in a hundred of completing the activity in less than this time.

Pessimistic Time

This is the longest time the activity could ever take, assuming that everything goes badly. The activity might be expected to exceed this time only once in one hundred times.

Most Likely Time

If the activity could be repeated many times under exactly the same conditions, this is the time that it would take more often than any other time. The most likely time is the estimate the manager would probably give if asked for a single time estimate.

To show the meaning of the three time estimates, imagine the

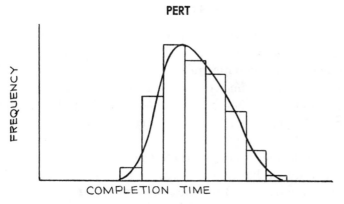

Fig. 10–2. Frequency Distribution of Activity Times

same activity repeated many times under the same conditions. Since this is an activity that is subject to chance, we will not complete it in the same duration each try. In Fig. 10–2, the horizontal axis shows the various times in which the activity was completed. The height of each bar shows how many times the activity was finished in that particular time. If we draw a smooth curve through the tops of the bars, we obtain what is called a *frequency distribution* curve for the duration of this activity.

The curve helps us to understand what is meant by the three time estimates, *a*, *b*, and *m*. The peak of the curve is *m*, the most likely time, and the two extremes of the curve are the optimistic and pessimistic times, respectively. (See Fig. 10–3.) Note that

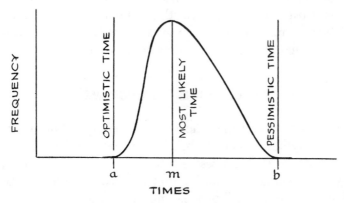

Fig. 10–3. Theoretical Frequency Distribution Curve for Activity Times

the curve is not necessarily symmetrical—m need not fall in the center between a and b.

In practice, the activities in PERT are almost never repeated many times in the manner described above. However, the three "educated guesses," when made by people who are familiar with the work, do permit us to know something about how such a curve *might* look.

To illustrate the use of the three time estimates, consider the simple activity of hanging a picture. Perhaps the most likely time for this activity is 3 minutes. If everything goes smoothly, and the nail grips the wall the first time, and the picture hangs straight without repeated adjustment, the job might be done in 2 minutes. On the other hand, if the nail does not hold, or the hammer hits the thumb, the job might take as long as 10 minutes. These would be examples of most likely, optimistic, and pessimistic times, respectively.

Use of optimistic, pessimistic, and most likely time estimates permits us to apply the theory of probability to projects where there is a good deal of uncertainty about how long each activity will take. Even though we do not know how long each *activity* can take, we can still come up with a prediction of how long the *project* will take. Moreover, we can predict the *chances* (probability) of completing the project in any given time.

Note that these three guesses are not based on different levels of resources (as was the case with the two time estimates used in Least-Cost Scheduling). All three guesses are based on doing the job the same way, with the same number of men, and represent the range of possibilities depending on chance.

RULES FOR ESTIMATING TIME

PERT is based on the science of *probability*. You don't have to know anything about probability or statistics in order to use PERT, but you should observe a few simple rules in making the three time estimates, in order that the laws of probability will hold and the results will be meaningful.

1. The most important rule to remember is that the estimates must not be influenced by the time available in which to complete

the project. Therefore, ignore any known dates or schedules.

2. The second rule is that each activity must be considered by itself, independent of any other activity. In other words, the time for installing a pump should not be increased to allow for the possibility of a late delivery of the pump. Rather, the uncertainty in delivery should be shown in the times for "deliver pump"; the time for installation should be determined independently.

To insure that conditions (1) and (2) are met, certain techniques may be used:

a) "Jumping around"—obtaining estimates for activities in different parts of the network in completely random fashion, rather than estimating the activities in their logical order.

b) Withholding contract or scheduled dates until after the time estimates have been prepared.

3. The time estimates must not be biased. Therefore, when dealing with foremen and supervisors, be sure to explain the meaning of the three estimates carefully. Make it clear that these are estimates and not schedules to which they are committed. This will help maintain an atmosphere conducive to honest, realistic estimates.

4. The pessimistic time is the longest time the activity might take under unfavorable conditions. It does *not* include an allowance for fires, floods, earthquakes, and other "acts of God." On the other hand, where the activity is subject to delays because of weather, the time of year should be considered, and the estimates should properly reflect the variations that might be expected in weather for that time of year. Thus, the optimistic time would reflect the planner's estimate if very good weather is experienced, and the pessimistic estimate, the effect of very bad weather (but not, for example, a typhoon or hurricane).

EXPECTED TIME, t_e

With the time estimates determined, PERT uses a weighted average of the three times to find the overall project duration. This average is called the *expected time*, t_e, and is found by the following simple formula:

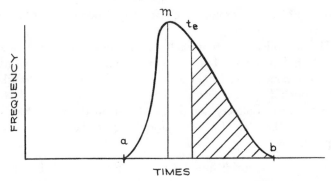

Fig. 10–4. Frequency Distribution Curve Illustrating t_e

$$t_e = \frac{a + 4m + b}{6}$$

To understand the meaning of t_e, consider the frequency distribution curve shown earlier for a typical activity, and repeated in Fig. 10–4.

A vertical line drawn at t_e divides the area under the curve into two equal parts. That is, if the activity were repeated many times, about half the time it would be completed in more time than t_e, and about half the time, in less time. Note that t_e is *not* necessarily the same as m, the most likely time.

The advantage of the weighted average (t_e) is that we can use it just as we did a single time estimate in CPM, to find the earliest and latest times, and the critical path.

FINDING EARLIEST AND LATEST TIMES

In PERT, we are interested in finding the earliest and latest occurrence times of *events*. The *earliest time* of occurrence of an event is called T_E, and *latest time* of occurrence is called T_L. To find the earliest time (T_E) of any event, simple add up the t_e's along the various paths leading to it. The longest path determines T_E. As with CPM, assume the time of occurrence (T_E) of the starting event to be zero. Simply add t_e to the time of occurrence of the preceding event to find the time of occurrence of the following event. If there is more than one possibility, choose the largest.

ILLUSTRATION OF PERT COMPUTATIONS

Consider the simple network shown in Fig. 10–5. The three time estimates have been written along the arrows. To find the expected time (t_e) for activity 1–2, we use the formula:

$$t_e = \frac{a + 4m + b}{6} = \frac{(1) + 4(2) + (3)}{6} = \frac{12}{6} = 2$$

Similarly, we find the expected times for the remaining activities in the same way. These are shown on the network in Fig. 10–6:

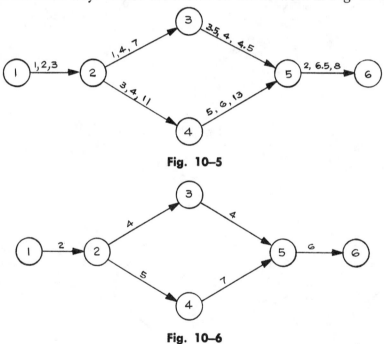

Fig. 10–5

Fig. 10–6

By performing the "forward pass" in the same manner as for CPM, we can find the earliest time, T_E, at which each event may be expected to occur. To start the computations, set T_E for event $(1) = 0$. From Fig. 10–6, T_E for event (2) is $0 + 2 = 2$.

In general, if i is the preceding and j the following event:

$$T_E (j) = T_E (i) + t_e (i\text{-}j)$$

At event (5), there are two possibilities; along the upper path, $T_E = 6 + 4 = 10$; and along the lower path $7 + 7 = 14$. We choose the larger figure. The earliest times (T_E's) are shown along the network in Fig. 10–7.

Similarly, by working backward through the network, start-

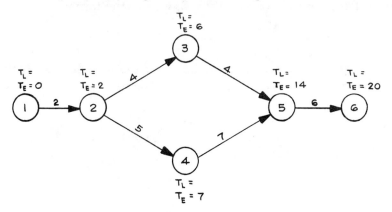

Fig. 10–7

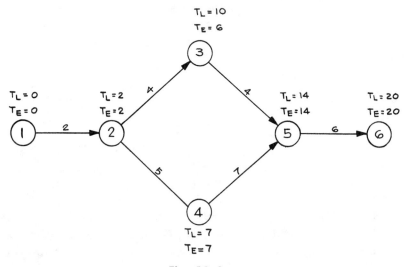

Fig. 10–8

ing with the last event, we can find the *latest time*, T_L, for each event. (As we have done with CPM, we have set $T_L = T_E$ for the last event.) Here, the formula is:

$$T_L (i) = T_L (j) - t_e (i\text{-}j)$$

Where there is more than one path, the smallest T_L is used. For event (5):

$$T_L = 20 - 6 = 14$$

For event (2), there are two possibilities. T_L, as computed along the upper path, from (3) to (2) is $10 - 4 = 6$ and from event (4) is $7 - 5 = 2$. We select the smallest value, 2, for T_L. Figure 10–8 shows the completed computations.

SLACK TIME

At any event, the difference between T_L and T_E is called *slack* and is a measure of the leeway available in completing the project. Slack time is similar to float, but while float time is asso-

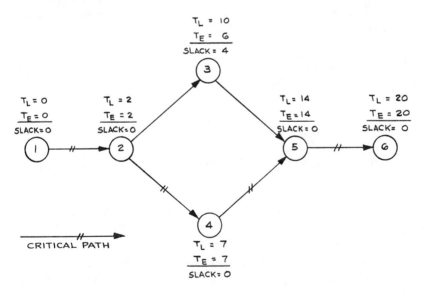

Fig. 10–9

ciated with an *activity,* slack time is always associated with an *event.* (Some texts use slack time to refer to both kinds of leeway, and use the term *activity slack* for what we have called float time.) Slack time is the time that an event can be delayed without affecting the earliest completion time (T_E) of the entire project. Figure 10–9 shows the network with earliest times (T_E), latest times (T_L), and event slack time. Events having zero slack lie on the critical path.

Event slack is easily computed, but it is not always as useful in project scheduling as (activity) float time. An event is just a point in time. It is the *activities* that really take up time and must be scheduled. Hence, we need to know the leeway associated with an activity.

FINDING THE CRITICAL PATH IN PERT

In the example of Fig. 10–9, we located the critical path by joining the critical events—those events with zero slack. Strictly speaking, the critical path is determined by the critical *activities* rather than the events. In Fig. 10–10, events (1), (2), (3), (4), and (5) are critical, but activity 2–4 is not critical; the critical path runs through 1–2–3–4–5.

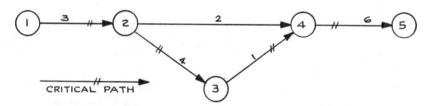

Fig. 10–10. Critical Path Determined by Critical Activities

PERT COMPUTATIONS USING GRAPHICAL SYMBOLS

The graphical symbols introduced in Chapter 6 are particularly useful for PERT computations. Once the three time estimates have been replaced by t_e, T_E and T_L are found directly. T_E is shown in the left half of each event bubble and T_L in the

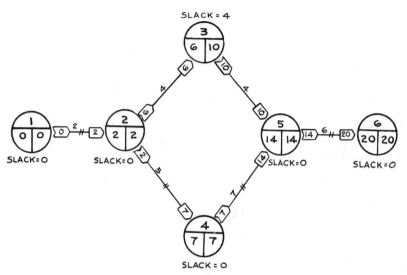

Fig. 10–11. Sample Problem Showing Graphical Symbols for the Computations

right half of the bubble. Figure 10–11 shows the completed sample problem of Fig. 10–9 using the graphical symbols.

In Chapter 6, float time was shown in a circle on the activity lines; however, in PERT we are dealing with slack (which is associated with events) and this symbol is not used. As a matter of fact, it is not really necessary to show the slack, since it can be readily determined by inspection by comparing the figure in the left-hand half with that in the right-hand half of the bubble. If these figures are the same, the event is critical; there is zero slack.

COMPUTATIONS USING THE WORK SHEET

PERT computations may also be done on a work sheet like that used for computing earliest and latest starting times in CPM. Here T_E for any event is simply the earliest start time of the following activities, and T_L is the smallest of the latest start times of the following activities. To find the event slack, subtract

Events		Expected Time t_e	ES	EF	LS	LF	T_E	T_L	Event Slack
i	j								
1	2	2	0	2	0	2	0	0	0*
2	3	4	2	6	6	10	2	2	0*
2	4	5	2	7	2	7			
3	5	4	6	10	10	14	6	10	4
4	5	7	7	14	7	14	7	7	0*
5	6	6	14	20	14	20	14	14	0*
6			20		20		20	20	0*

ES = Early Start
EF = Early Finish
LS = Late Start
LF = Late Finish

T_E = Earliest (event) time
T_L = Latest (event) time
i = Preceding event
j = Following event

*Critical event.

Fig. 10–12. PERT Work Sheet

T_E from T_L. The work sheet of Fig. 10–12 shows the computations for the sample problem. T_E and T_L refer to the preceding event (i).

STANDARD DEVIATION AND VARIANCE OF AN ACTIVITY

The three time estimates of PERT can be used to tell us something about the degree of uncertainty involved in the activity. For example, consider two activities with frequency distribution curves as shown in Fig. 10–13. It is obvious that there is much

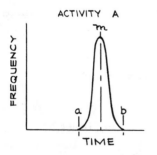
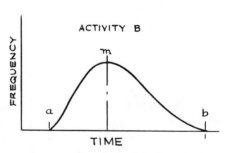

Fig. 10–13. Activities with Different Frequency Distributions

more uncertainty about how long activity B will take than about activity A. (As a matter of fact, in the case of A a single time estimate would probably be used.) A measure of the "spread" of the distribution is called the *standard deviation* and is shown by the Greek letter sigma (σ). The standard deviation can be found (approximately) from the following very simple formula:

$$\sigma = \frac{b - a}{6}$$

We can use the standard deviation to tell us about the chances of reaching any event by a certain date. To do this, we must introduce one more term. This is the *variance, v.* The variance is simply the square of the standard deviation:

$$v = \sigma^2 = \left(\frac{b - a}{6}\right)^2$$

The variance is useful because of a peculiar property that we shall illustrate later.

Since the duration of each of the activities in the network (t_e) is uncertain, the time of occurrence of each event (T_E) is also subject to uncertainty. The event could actually occur over a range of time as shown by a frequency distribution curve like the one in Fig. 10–14.

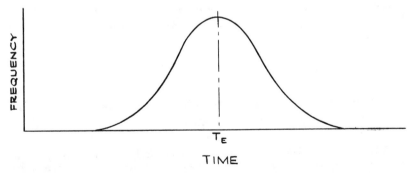

Fig. 10–14. Frequency Distribution Curve for Event Time (T_E)

A peculiar feature of this curve is that although the distribution curves of the individual activities were not necessarily symmetrical, the distribution curve for the event time is symmetrical about T_E.* This is true if there are at least several (say four or more) activities in the chain ahead of the event. A symmetrical distribution of this type is called a *normal distribution*. It is also often called a *bell curve* because of its shape. It is this fact—that the distribution curve for T_E tends to take the shape of the bell curve—that permits us to estimate the probability of finishing the job on time. How this is done will be shown shortly.

Like the activity, the event times also can have a wide or narrow "spread." The spread of the activities is also measured by the *standard deviation*, σ_{T_E}, and the *variance*, V. We can find the variance of the event time by adding up the variances of the activities along the longest path leading to that activity. This is the valuable property of activity variances to which we referred earlier.

We shall use a small v to designate the variance of an activity and a capital V to mean the variance of an event. To find the standard deviation of an event, we recall that it is the square root of the variance:

$$\sigma_{T_E} = \sqrt{V}$$

The "spread" of the bell curve is measured by the standard deviation σ_{T_E}. Although we cannot find the standard deviation directly, we can find the variance (V) by summing up the variances of individual activities along the longest path leading to that event. The standard deviation is then the square root of this sum:

$$\sigma_{T_E} = \sqrt{V} = \sqrt{v_{1-2} + v_{2-3} \ldots v_{ij}}$$

Where there is more than one path having equal times, use the one with the largest sum of variances.

---

* Why this curve should approximate a symmetrical "bell curve" may not be too clear. However, this can be derived from the Central Limit Theorem of statistical theory. The interested reader is referred to textbooks on this subject.

CHARACTERISTICS OF THE NORMAL DISTRIBUTION

The normal distribution (bell curve) is found often in nature, wherever there is a random or chance distribution of some vari-

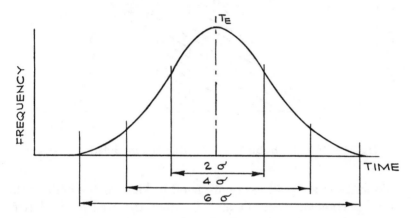

Fig. 10–15. Characteristics of the Normal Distribution

able factor. Among its characteristics are the following (Fig. 10–15):

1. Sixty-eight per cent of the area under the curve lies within a spread of 2σ.
2. A width equal to 4σ takes in 96 per cent of the area of the curve.
3. A width of 6σ includes practically all the area under the curve.

PROBABILITY OF COMPLETION BY A SCHEDULED DATE

The curve in Fig. 10–16 shows the normal distribution for T_E. Let us assume that we are scheduled to complete the project by some date, T_S. Imagine that the area under the curve represents 100 per cent. The chance (probability) of completing by T_S is equal to the area under the curve to the left of T_S. The area under the curve to the right of T_S represents the probability that the job will not be completed by T_S.

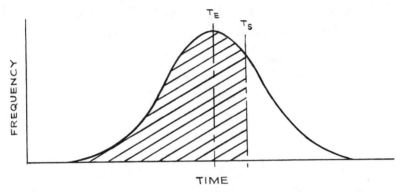

Fig. 10–16. Probability of Meeting a Scheduled Date—T_S

To find the area, all we really need to know is the area of the shaded portion between T_E and T_S, since the area to the left of T_E is equal to 50 per cent. To find this area, we must express the difference between T_E and T_S in terms of σ_{T_E}, the standard deviation. This difference is called the *deviation* and is denoted by z. It is found by the simple formula:

$$z = \frac{T_S - T_E}{\sigma_{T_E}}$$

For example, suppose the difference between T_S and T_E is equal to one sigma. Then the area under the curve to the left of T_S is 84 per cent, and there is an 84 per cent chance of completing the project by T_S. Knowing z, we can find the area under the curve from standard tables that are found in books on statistics. However, for most PERT purposes, a simplified table such as Table 10–1 will suffice.

A probability of 76.32 per cent may have meaning in statistical or actuarial work, but in PERT the probability serves merely as a guide to management on the likelihood of completing by a specified date. For this purpose, a figure of 75 or 76 per cent is entirely adequate.

TABLE 10–1

PERT Probability Table

$z = \dfrac{T_S - T_E}{\sigma_{T_E}}$	Probability of Completing by T_S	$z = \dfrac{T_S - T_E}{\sigma_{T_E}}$	Probability of Completing by T_S
−3.0	0	+ .1	.54
−2.5	.01	+ .2	.58
−2.0	.03	+ .3	.62
−1.5	.07	+ .4	.66
−1.4	.08	+ .5	.69
−1.3	.09	+ .6	.73
−1.2	.11	+ .7	.76
−1.1	.14	+ .8	.79
−1.0	.16	+ .9	.82
− .9	.18	+1.0	.84
− .8	.21	+1.1	.86
−. 7	.24	+1.2	.88
− .6	.27	+1.3	.90
− .5	.31	+1.4	.92
−. 4	.35	+1.5	.93
− .3	.38	+2.0	.98
− .2	.42	+2.5	.99
− .1	.46	+3.0	1.00
0	.50		

The probability is based on the planned method of accomplishment of the project, with no expediting. If it is too low, management may add resources to critical activities, in order to reduce their times. On the other hand, if the probability of reaching the desired completion date is very high, perhaps resources are being wasted. Note also that the probability is associated with an *event*, not with an activity.

It is also possible to work backward and use PERT to set a schedule. Once the variance and standard deviations are known, one can select any desired level of probability, find the corresponding z from the table, and then substitute in the formula:

$$z = \frac{T_S - T_E}{\sigma_{T_E}}$$

to find T_S.

ILLUSTRATION OF PROBABILITIES

In the simple example given previously, the critical path was 1–2, 2–4, 4–5, and 4–6, and the expected time for the project, (T_E), 20 working days. To find the variance in the project completion time, we must sum up the variances along the critical path. We start by finding the standard deviation (σ) for the critical activities using the formula:

$$\sigma = \frac{b - a}{6}$$

Activity $i - j$	Estimated Times: Optimistic a	Estimated Times: Most Likely m	Estimated Times: Pessimistic b	Expected Time $t_e = \frac{a + 4m + b}{6}$	Critical Operation	Standard Deviation $\sigma = \frac{b-a}{6}$	Variance $v = \sigma^2$
1–2	1	2	3	2	x	1/3	1/9
2–3	1	4	7	4			
2–4	3	4	11	5	x	4/3	16/9
3–5	3.5	4.0	4.5	4			
4–5	5	6	13	7	x	4/3	16/9
5–6	2	6.5	8	6	x	3/3	9/9

$$V = \Sigma v^{*} = \frac{42}{9} = 4.67$$

* The Greek letter Σ (*Sigma*) means "the sum of."

Fig. 10–17. Computing Variance, V

We then square the standard deviation to find the variance, and finally add up the variances along the critical path to find V_{T_E}, the variance of the end event. This is shown above in Fig. 10–17.

The standard deviation will be the square root of the variance:

$$\sigma = \sqrt{V} = \sqrt{4.67} = \text{approximately } 2.16$$

Figure 10–18 shows the distribution function (curve) for this time (T_E). The project will most probably be finished some-

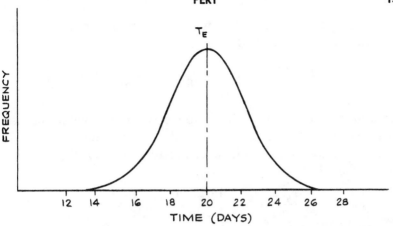

Fig. 10–18. Frequency Distribution of Time of End Event

where between days 18 and 22, but there is a remote possibility that it may be completed as early as day 14 or as late as day 26.

Suppose we want to know the probability of completing by day 21. (See Fig. 10–19.) From the diagram, there is a 50–50 chance of completing by day 20. The chances of completion by day 21 are better than 50 per cent. To find out how much better, we find the difference between the scheduled time (T_S) and T_E.

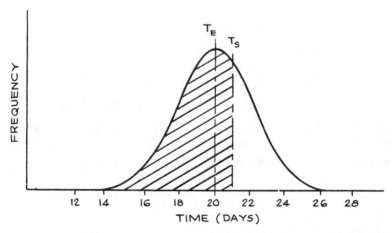

Fig. 10–19. Probability of Completion by Scheduled Date T_S

This is $21 - 20 = 1$ day. We then express this in terms of σ_{T_E}, the standard deviation, to find z:

$$z = \frac{T_S - T_E}{\sigma_{T_E}} = \frac{21 - 20}{2.16} = \frac{+1}{2.16} = +.463$$

Look up z in Table 10-1. The probability of completing by day 21 is between .66 and .69. Let us call it 68 per cent.

What is the probability of completing by day 19, one day sooner than T_E?

$$z = \frac{T_S - T_E}{\sigma_{T_E}} = \frac{19 - 20}{2.16} = \frac{-1}{2.16} = -.46$$

Note that z is *negative* because T_S is earlier than T_E. Looking at Table 10-1 for $z = -.46$, we find that the probability is only about 33 per cent. This means there is only one chance in three that the project will be finished by day 19.

Suppose now that we want to select a completion date for which the probability of completion will be at least 85 per cent. Referring to Table 10-1, we find that 85 per cent probability falls between $z = 1.0$ and $z = 1.1$. By interpolation, we say that $z = 1.05$ for a probability of 85 per cent.

$$z = \frac{T_S - T_E}{\sigma_{T_E}}$$

$$1.05 = \frac{T_S - 20}{2.16}$$

$$T_S - 20 = 2.16 \times (1.05)$$

$$T_S = 20 + 2.16 \times (1.05) = 20 + 2.26 = 22.26$$

Solving this equation, we find $T_S = 22.26$. A practical scheduled date is the next round number, day 23, which will give better than an 85 per cent chance of successful completion.

PERT VS. CPM

Now that we understand the principles of PERT, we can review it in relation to CPM. Both systems employ the same basic technique of arrow diagramming. PERT uses three time esti-mates in a statistical approach to times. This is called *probabilistic*. CPM deals with jobs where times are more readily deter-mined and uses a single time estimate. This approach is called *deterministic*. Both systems locate the critical path in much the same way. Traditionally, PERT is event-oriented, while CPM concentrates on activities. However, it is possible to have ac-tivity-oriented PERT and event-oriented CPM.

By concentrating on activities, CPM makes it possible to asso-ciate a specific cost with each activity. It is much more diffi-cult to associate a cost with an event, which is merely a point in time. Development of a least-cost schedule, as was done in Chapter 9, usually requires the CPM approach.

Finally, PERT permits use of the probability theory to tell something about the chances of completing by any given date.

The characteristics of PERT and CPM are compared in Table 10–2.

TABLE 10–2

Comparison of PERT and CPM

Characteristic	PERT	CPM
Network diagram	Usually event-oriented	Usually activity-oriented
Type of activities for which suitable	Probabilistic (durations are uncertain)	Deterministic (durations can be estimated)
Time estimates	Multiple estimates	Single estimate
Least-cost scheduling	Not very feasible	Yes
Probability of meeting a scheduled date	Yes	No

PERT was originally developed for control and reporting of complex research and development projects. The system was event-oriented because management was concerned with im-portant "milestones" such as completion dates and deliveries of the various systems and components, rather than with the activi-ties necessary to their completion. The multiple time estimate was used because of the uncertainty associated with completing the activities.

Knowledge of PERT is essential to aerospace contractors and manufacturers since it is a requirement of most government contracts. Construction contractors may also find PERT specified by a particular owner or general contractor. In some cases a PERT computer program that you can utilize may be available. To adapt a PERT program to CPM, simply use the same time estimate for a, m, and b.

PERT can be used to good advantage in planning and control of any project involving uncertainty such as in research programs, or unusual design and construction projects. In construction, PERT would also apply to activities that are very susceptible to delay by weather, high water, etc. It would also be used for excavation where the subsurface conditions are not known. In general, however, most construction men have found that the extra refinement of PERT's three time estimates is not required for construction work.

PERT involves more computations than does CPM, and for large projects a computer is almost mandatory, especially if computation of variance is also required. For smaller projects, an inexpensive slide rule is available to convert the three time estimates to a single expected time. From this point on, the manual computations may be done in a manner similar to CPM either directly on the network or on a work sheet.

EVENT-ORIENTED VS. ACTIVITY-ORIENTED NETWORKS

A few comments are appropriate on the choice of event-oriented vs. activity-oriented networks. Activity-oriented networks are most applicable at the lowest operating level where control of individual jobs is the major concern. At the higher levels of management, there is more interest in meeting key completion dates and other "milestones" and hence an event-oriented network may be more suitable. A little practice with each type of network will enable the manager to pick the one that suits his needs best.

Much of the original literature on PERT was event-oriented to such an extent that it recommended drawing the diagram by considering the events. For example, for construction of a house, some PERT texts recommended starting with the end event, "house completed," and working backward through the network.

The procedure of drawing a network by starting with the events and then trying to fill in the activities is not recommended. First of all, it is quite possible to have a network that shows all the events in the project, but omits one or more activities. Second, concentrating on the events when drawing the network may obscure certain important relationships between the activities, such as overlapping (see Chapter 3). In any project, it is the activities that are the real happenings; events are only man-made concepts determined by the beginning or end of the activities. It is the activities that must be accomplished to complete the project.

For these reasons, even if an event-oriented PERT diagram is desired, start by drawing the *activities* in their correct sequence. Once the activities have been correctly shown you can identify the events and label them for emphasis. Starting with the events alone and trying to fill in the activities is likely to lead to erroneous results.

OBJECTIONS TO PERT

A number of objections have been raised to PERT in recent years. Some of these are based on practical considerations—the difficulty involved in preparing three time estimates (including the tendency to estimate m, and then to "fudge" a and b by spacing them equally on either side of m), plus the complexity of the probability calculations. Others have questioned the theoretical assumptions that are behind the PERT formulas. A further objection is the fact that PERT seems to provide a "rubber yardstick" when it comes to controlling the execution of the project.

Although some of these objections are valid, PERT continues to be used, particularly by aerospace contractors. Moreover, in spite of theoretical weaknesses, it continues to produce useful results. With the type of data that is usually available, a more refined and mathematically exact system is probably not justified.

The single time estimate approach of CPM is probably satisfactory for most projects, particularly in the construction field.

Familiarity with PERT is desirable, however, both to satisfy government requirements, and also for unusual projects such as research and development where the probabilistic approach may be justified.

PROBLEMS

10–1. One step in preparing a passenger aircraft for flight is cleaning the cabin. This usually takes 29 minutes for a crew of three. However, it has been done in as little as 24 minutes, and on occasion has required 33 minutes:

    a) What is the expected time (t_e) for cleaning the aircraft cabin?

    b) What is the standard deviation (σ) for this operation?

    c) What is the variance (v) associated with this operation?

10–2. The following are the PERT time estimates for three activities in a project. For which activity is the uncertainty the greatest?

    Activity 1: $a = 4,\ m = 12,\ b = 16$

    Activity 2: $a = 33,\ m = 37,\ b = 40$

    Activity 3: $a = 12,\ m = 18,\ b = 26$

10–3. In planning for a live television program, the producer lists the following important events. Draw an event-oriented PERT network using these events.

Event	Description
1	Start project
2	Director selected
3	Script completed
4	Start casting
5	Scenery design completed
6	Costumes selected
7	Casting completed
8	Rehearsal completed
9	Scenery ready
10	On-air

10–4. Figure 10–20 is part of the PERT network for a large project.

    a) What is the earliest event time, T_E, for event 5?

    b) Compute the variance, v, for each activity.

    c) What is the variance (V) associated with the event time (T_E) of event 5?

    d) What is the standard deviation (σ) associated with the event time (T_E) of event 5?

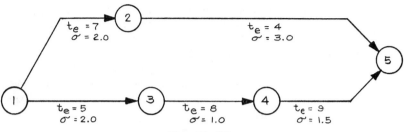

Fig. 10–20

10–5. The recipe for cooking a roast recommends 30 minutes, but experience has shown that more or less time may be required, depending on the quality of the meat, type of cut, oven temperature, etc. If the completion time (T_E) follows a normal distribution with the mean $T_E = 30$ minutes and $\sigma = 3$ minutes:

    a) What per cent of the time will the roast be properly done if left in the oven for just 30 minutes each time?

    b) What are the chances of the roast being ready if it is taken out after 28 minutes?

    c) What chance is there that the roast will *not* be ready if it is left in for 35 minutes?

    d) What per cent of the time will the roast require less than 24 minutes or more than 36 minutes cooking time?

10–6. Given the PERT network and time estimates in Fig. 10–21:

    a) Compute the expected time, t_e, for each activity.

    b) Compute T_E (the earliest time) and T_L (the latest time), and determine the event slack for all events.

    c) Identify the critical path.

    d) What is the probability of reaching event 5 by day 10?

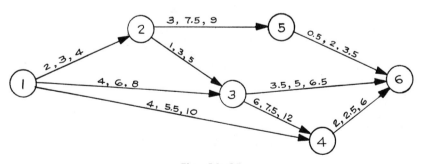

Fig. 10–21

e) What is the earliest completion time of the project?

f) What are the chances of reaching event 4 by day 13?

Note:
$$\sqrt{\frac{14}{9}} = 1.25$$

g) The contract schedule allows 18 days in which to complete the entire project. What are the chances that we will *not* finish on time?

Note:
$$\sqrt{2} = 1.41$$

11

Project Control and
Reporting Procedures

In Chapter 1, we defined CPM as a tool for planning, scheduling, and control. So far, we have covered use of CPM (and PERT) in scheduling and planning. This chapter will consider the third aspect: the use of these methods during the project execution stage, including progress control and reporting; updating the network; cost reporting; and progress payments. The discussion will center on CPM, but the principles are equally applicable if PERT is used.

PROGRESS CONTROL

Progress control includes constant monitoring to insure that each operation is completed on schedule and the taking of corrective action in case of slippages. The steps involved are:

1. Reporting job progress.
2. Comparing actual with scheduled progress.
3. Taking appropriate corrective action when required.

PROGRESS REPORTING

Every manager requires some means for keeping track of job progress. In addition, some type of report is usually required by management, client, owner, etc. In many current Department of Defense and NASA contracts, procedures for progress reporting are spelled out in great detail. In the absence of such specifications each company should select its own form of reporting, taking into consideration the type of job, the preferences of its own management, and the requirements of the owner or prime contractor.

With projects scheduled by CPM, three methods are commonly used:

1. Recording job progress on the network diagram.
2. Recording progress on a network diagram drawn to a time scale (modified bar chart).
3. Noting progress on a tabular schedule form.

Use of Network Diagram

The network diagram can be used as a record of progress by applying one or a combination of the following techniques as each operation is completed:

1. Color in the appropriate arrow using colored pencil, "dry-marker," or colored tape.
2. Draw a diagonal line through the bubble, marking completion of an event.
3. Note the actual completion dates on the diagram.

Scheduled dates should be shown on the network; actual dates may then be compared to these to insure that there has been no slippage. Progress should be checked at regular weekly, bi-weekly, or monthly intervals. If the chart is kept up to date, it can also serve as the basis for preparing reports to higher management.

Modified Bar Chart

Some companies make a practice of redrawing the network to a time-scale, thus combining the features of a bar chart and a network. This procedure is recommended only for condensed summary charts to be used for reporting to higher levels of management. At the working level it is usually too tedious and time-consuming. Also, in the event of schedule changes, the entire chart may have to be redrawn.

To show progress using this type of chart, the arrows are colored in, or a bar of contrasting color or pattern is drawn adjacent to the arrow to show the extent of completion. A vertical line is drawn showing the time "now" (date of report) against which progress is compared. This type of chart was illustrated in Chapter 7, Fig. 7-3 (page 74).

Tabular Reports and Schedules

A schedule or list of operations can also be used for progress control and reporting.

The CPM work sheet (Chapter 5) produces a list of all the operations with their earliest and latest starting and completion dates. Similar tabulations are provided by electronic computers. In either case, the tabulation can be used to record job progress by entering actual dates on the schedule as each operation is started or completed.

Figure 11–1 shows part of a tabular schedule for construction of a highway overpass. For simplicity, earliest and latest dates have been omitted, and the list shows only the *scheduled* starting and completion dates. Day numbers have been translated into calendar dates for the convenience of field personnel. (See Chapter 7.) Operation 020–030 is scheduled for completion on February 25. Since this falls within the reporting period (week ending February 26), it is checked in color. Likewise, operation 030–060, which is supposed to start on February 26, is flagged for the attention of the field supervisor. At the end of the week, the supervisor will enter the actual dates for these two activities in the columns provided.

REPORTS TO MANAGEMENT

The same charts or schedules used for checking on job progress may also be used for reports to higher management. More usually, however, some type of a summary report is used. Graphical progress charts offer many advantages. If the chart is kept up-to-date by showing actual completions, a progress re-

PROJECT: HIGH STREET OVERPASS
CONTRACTOR: SMITH BROTHERS CONSTRUCTION COMPANY

WEEK ENDING: 2/26/X2

Critical	Activity i	j	Description	Duration	Scheduled Start	Scheduled Finish	Float	Actual Start	Actual Finish	Remarks
*	010	020	Deliver Pile Rig	3	2/15	2/17	0	2/15	2/17	
	010	040	Deliver Piles	10	3/9	3/22	1			
* √	020	030	Prepare Site	5	2/18	2/25	0	2/18		
* √	030	060	Excav. Ftg., Bent. #2	2	2/26	3/1	0			
	040	050	Drive Piles, Bent. #1	3	3/23	3/25	1			
*	060	070	Form Ftg., Bent. #2	1	3/2	3/2	0			
	060	110	Excav. Ftg., Bent. #3	2	3/23	3/24	1			
*	070	080	Pour Conc. Ftg., Bent. #2	1	3/3	3/3	0			
*	080	090	Form Bent. #2	6	3/4	3/11	0			
	110	120	Form Ftg., Bent. #3	1	3/18	3/18	6			
	050	150	Form Pile Cap, Bent. #1	1	3/26	3/26	1			

Fig. 11-1. Job Progress Record, Using Tabular Schedule

port can be submitted as often as desired, simply by reproducing the marked-up chart.

Tabular reports have the advantage of convenient size and may cover more detail. The fact is, however, that few people—and few executives—will take time to wade through many pages and columns of closely printed tabular data.

Regardless of the form it takes, the report should highlight delays and slippages according to the principle of "management by exception." It should be accompanied by comments as to the cause of the delays, and action being taken or proposed to bring the project back to schedule.

FOLLOW-UP

Progress reporting alone is of little value without effective follow-up. If a delay occurs in a non-critical activity, corrective action will usually be limited to rescheduling the following non-critical activities. These operations must now be watched more closely, since part of their float time has been used up and they may easily become critical. If a delay occurs in one of the critical activities, corrective action would include the procedures discussed in Chapters 7 and 8 such as adding additional resources, trade-offs from non-critical to critical operations, rescheduling of series operations in parallel, etc. If the time cannot be made up by any of these methods, completion of the project will be delayed.

UPDATING

It is rare that a project proceeds exactly in accordance with the schedule. The CPM network is a blueprint for a project to be accomplished some time in the future. Although based on the best possible judgment about the nature of work, it is only a prediction. As the work progresses, the assumptions used in planning may be justified or may require changing. Operations will be completed ahead of or behind schedule. New operations may be found necessary; some operations may turn out to be unnecessary and may be deleted. Problems thought to be serious may prove to be minor, while, on the other hand, unsuspected bottlenecks may develop. An alert manager is always on the lookout for shortcuts or opportunities to telescope operations. All of these factors may require changes to the time estimates or to the sequence of operations shown on the network.

The process of keeping the network up-to-date is called *updating*. It is closely tied in with progress reporting, but whereas progress reporting is concerned with recording actual completions and comparing them with the schedule, updating takes into consideration all of the changes in the project, including changes in the sequence of operations. Progress reporting deals with *past* performance: those operations that have been completed. Updating refers to scheduling of *future* operations and of the project completion in the light of past progress.

Like the initial CPM analysis, updating follows a definite sequence of steps: First, the network is corrected to show the effects of delays and changes in the sequence of operations or in the time estimates. Then, the computations are repeated to find the effect of these changes on the critical path and the completion time. Finally, adjustments are made that result in a new set of CPM schedules to control the remainder of the project.

Updating computations are similar to the initial computations (Chapters 5 and 6) with certain exceptions: The computations should be started at the present time, rather than at time zero. (The "present time" would be the date of the most recent progress report.) The day number of the "present time" is used as the *earliest start time* for all the beginning operations of the network, instead of zero.

For operations that have been partially completed, the number of days *remaining to complete* is used as the duration. Operations that have been 100 per cent completed are listed if necessary to preserve the continuity of the diagram, but their durations are shown as zero. Operations that have not yet been started are shown at their proper durations, reflecting the latest estimate.

During the course of the project, firm delivery dates are generally established for many items. At the time of updating, these dates should be used in place of the previous estimates by converting the known calendar date to a day number, and entering this day number as the *earliest finish date* of that operation. An estimate of duration is no longer required for such deliveries.

ILLUSTRATION OF UPDATING COMPUTATIONS

The difference between updating computations and those for a new CPM network may be shown by a simple example. Figure 11–2 shows a simple project network with the original time

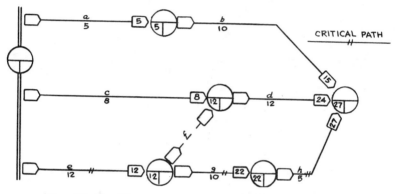

Fig. 11–2. Illustration of Updating Computations

estimates. (*Note:* In this and the other illustrations in this chapter, a *base line* [Chapter 2] is used instead of a single bubble for the starting event to avoid crowding and make the drawing more legible.) A quick computation of the "forward pass" (use the method of Chapter 6) shows that the project time is 27 days and the critical path runs through operations *e–g–h*.

At the end of the first 2 weeks (10 working days), the status of the project is as follows:

1. Operation *a* has been completed.
2. Operations *b* and *c* have been started, but are still in progress. The Project Manager estimates that it will require another 7 days to complete operation *b*, and 2 days to finish operation *c*.
3. Operation *e* is a delivery that was originally estimated to take

12 days. The item is now definitely scheduled to arrive on day 11.

4. Operation *g* was completed ahead of sequence.

5. Operations *d* and *h* have not yet been started, and there is no change in their time estimates.

Figure 11–3 shows the status of the project at the end of day 10. Note that the diagram is not to scale, but the length of the lines showing completion is made roughly proportional to the per cent of the operation that has been completed.

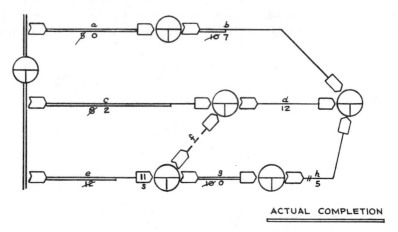

ACTUAL COMPLETION

Fig. 11–3. Illustrative Problem Showing Status at Day 10

The current status of each operation is shown as follows:

1. Since operation *a* has been completed, its effective time is shown as *zero*.

2. For operations *b* and *c*, the time required *to complete* is shown instead of the original estimate.

3. The delivery shown by operation *e* is now definitely scheduled to arrive on day 11. Since this date is fixed and is not dependent on any other operations, we enter it directly in the arrowhead (earliest finish date) for operation *e*. We also mark this day *s* to show that it is a scheduled date, independent of the CPM computations.

4. Although operation *g* has been completed, we cannot drop it, since to do so would break the continuity of the diagram. We do, however, reduce its time to *zero*.

5. Since there is no change in the estimated times for operations d and h, the original times are shown on the diagram.

Figure 11–4 shows the updating computations (forward pass only) using the revised durations from Fig. 11–3. In this case, we must start the computations from the time *now*, that is, the date of the report (day 10). This day becomes the earliest start

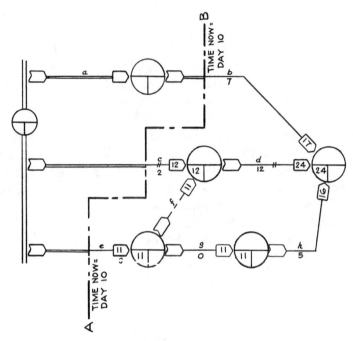

Fig. 11–4. Updating Computations—Forward Pass

date of operations b and c. This is shown graphically by the line A–B in Fig. 11–4. In effect, we ignore all operations to the left of this line. Thus, for the chain a–b, we ignore a, which was completed, and find the completion of b as:

$$10 + 7 = 17$$

For c, the earliest completion is

$$10 + 2 = 12$$

For operation e, the scheduled completion of day 11 is used.

Note that we do not add the "time now" in this case. Another way of looking at it is to say that since operation e will definitely be completed on day 11, and the "time now" is day 10, then the remaining duration for e is only 1 day. Either way, we find 11 as the earliest finish date for operation e, which is also the earliest starting date for the following operations, since no other arrows enter the bubble.

Continuing with the forward pass, we find that the project can now be finished on day 24, instead of day 27 as previously scheduled. The critical path has shifted from e-g-h to c-d.

Some comment may be in order about completing g before e. This seems to violate the basic rule of CPM that no operation can start until those preceding it have been completed. This is true. However, the network should reflect the true nature of the work; the work should not be chained to the network! What has happened here is that the original network was in error. Obviously, if operation g could be started and completed before e, it was not really dependent on e. It should have been shown as a parallel (independent) operation, as in Fig. 11–5.

In practice, it is not necessary to redraw the network as in Fig. 11–5. Operation g has already been completed and will not

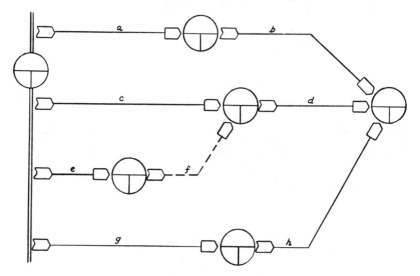

Fig. 11–5. Revised Network Showing Correct Relationships

affect the calculations. This is a general rule for updating: We are concerned only with the *remaining* operations in the project, not with those already completed.

FREQUENCY OF UPDATING

The frequency of updating depends on the extent of changes in the network. It should be done whenever major changes occur that will affect project completion or cause a shift in the critical path, or when the impact of changes on the schedule cannot be readily determined by inspecting the diagram. On the other hand, good judgment should be used and the network revised only when the changes and their effect on the schedule are significant. Too frequent revision results in wasted effort and confusion.

PROGRESS REPORTING USING ELECTRONIC COMPUTERS

The use of computers to help in the CPM calculations is discussed in detail in Chapters 13 and 14. Here we will mention their use in connection with progress reporting and updating.

If a computer (or a computer service) is available, it can speed up the process of updating and progress reporting. The following procedure has been used successfully by a number of companies in connection with widely scattered construction projects.

1. Once each week, on Friday afternoon, the Superintendent reviews his schedule and notes items completed, items delayed (for which a change in estimated time is necessary), or changes in the network.
2. This information is telephoned to the main office (or to the computer center directly) giving the event numbers of the activities involved.
3. The updating information is punched into cards and fed through the computer together with the original schedule. The computer produces an updated CPM schedule that is sent airmail special delivery and is available on the Superintendent's desk

by Monday morning. The revised schedule shows only the operations that remain to be done. It will reflect changes in completion time, shifts in the critical path, etc. Copies may be furnished to the main office for review, if desired.

A modification of the above system makes use of special data-transmitting equipment by means of which information can be sent over ordinary telephone lines direct to a receiving device at the computer center. The project field office is furnished with a deck of prepunched cards, representing each operation in the network. Each week the project manager or Superintendent pulls the cards for operations on which work was done during that week, and notes those that have been completed, or the number of days of work remaining on those only partly completed.

At a set time, the field clerk telephones the computer center and is connected directly with the receiving device. He then feeds the cards into the sending device, keying in the symbols either for completion or for the number of days remaining. The receiving device—an automatic key punch—produces a set of punched cards that are used as input to produce a new CPM schedule.

FISCAL REPORTING AND COST CONTROL

Another important area of project management is *cost control*. The cost of material and labor expended on a job is easily determined from accounting records. But, until the job is completed, it is difficult to determine with any accuracy whether the amount "earned," as measured by the work completed, is commensurate with the costs incurred to date. This problem is particularly acute in construction work, where it is difficult to assign a dollar value to partially completed work.

Many companies and government agencies have found that with CPM they can readily combine progress reporting with cost accounting and other fiscal controls,° including periodic requests

---

° The federal government has developed such a system—based on PERT—called PERT/Cost.

for payment. If the CPM arrow diagram was based on a cost estimate as recommended in Chapter 4, it is usually not too difficult to assign a specific cost to each operation. The resulting schedule now becomes the basis for cost reporting; and with approval by the owner, it can also serve to compute progress payments.

As each operation is completed, the project is "credited" with the dollar value of that operation. Operations in progress at the end of the month (or other reporting period) are credited with a portion of their cost based on the estimated per cent of completion. The sum of the dollar values of the operations completed or partly completed is the value of work put in place.

This type of cost report is shown in Fig. 11–6. Here the amounts in column 3 are taken from the original cost estimate or project budget. The percentages in column 4 are estimates as

CONTRACT: C-1097						DATE: Dec. 1, 19X1
Event Numbers i j (1)	Description (2)	Budgeted Amount ($) (3)	Per Cent Completed (%) (4)	Amount Earned ($) (5)	Amount Expended ($) (6)	Underrun or (Overrun) ($) (7)
105-107 107-109 87-93	Prepare Subgrade Place and Finish Basement Floor Slab Concrete Block Wall-South	800 1,800 2,400	100 0 50	800 0 1,200		
Total		305,000		140,000	155,000	(15,000)

Fig. 11–6.   Project Cost Report

of the reporting date. Since the operations are small in relation to the whole project, great precision in estimating the per cent complete is not important. Column 5 is found by multiplying columns 3 and 4.

The total of column 5 in Fig. 11–6 represents the "value" of that portion of the project completed to date. The figure in column 6 is the total actually spent on the project, as reported by the Accounting Department. The difference between these

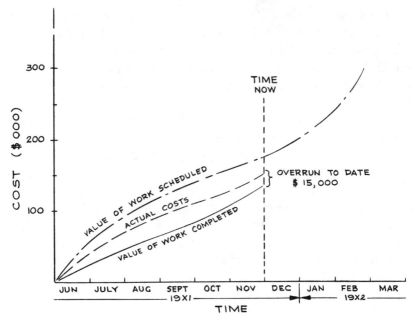

Fig. 11–7. Graph of Actual Expenditures vs. Value of Work Completed

two figures is shown in column 7. This tells us whether we are spending more or less than we should.

Figure 11–7 shows a cumulative graph in which the value of work completed is compared with actual costs expended. In this case, the cost of the work has been continually greater than the value of the work completed. As of December 1, we have completed $140,000 worth of work, but we have spent $155,000 to do so. This results in a cost "overrun" of $15,000.

Figure 11–7 also shows another curve representing the value of work *scheduled*. Since the value of work completed is less than the value of work scheduled, we can see that the project is not being completed as fast as planned. Of course, we must refer to the CPM schedule to find out just where and why the project is behind schedule. The type of graph shown in Fig. 11–7 makes an excellent summary of project cost status for higher management.

PROGRESS REPORTING UNDER A COST ACCOUNTING SYSTEM

The type of progress and cost report outlined in the preceding paragraphs is readily adaptable to a cost accounting system. With cost accounting, actual costs for labor and materials, and a proportionate share of overhead expense, are charged to *each operation*. These actual costs are then compared to the budgeted amounts for the operation.

A portion of a project cost report is shown in Fig. 11–8. This is the same as Fig. 11–6, except that actual costs are shown for each operation in column 5 rather than for the project as a whole as in the previous example. The difference between the value of work completed and the actual cost may now be computed for each operation, showing just where the overruns and underruns are found.

Because of the work required to charge actual labor and materials costs to the many operations, cost accounting systems of this type are not used by all companies. However, firms that do keep cost accounting records will find specific, clearly defined operations shown by the CPM arrows ideal for this type of cost analysis.

Event Numbers i j (1)	Description (2)	Budgeted Amount ($) (3)	Per Cent Completed (%) (4)	Amount Earned ($) (5)	Amount Expended ($) (6)	Underrun or (Overrun) ($) (7)
105-107	Prepare Subgrade	800	100	800	712	88
107-109	Place and Finish Basement Floor Slab	1,800	0	0	0	
87-93	Concrete Block Wall-South	2,400	50	1,200	2,000	(800)
	Total	305,000		140,000	155,000	(15,000)

CONTRACT: C-1097   DATE: Dec. 1, 19X1

Fig. 11–8. Project Cost Report Using Cost Accounting

PROGRESS PAYMENTS

The detailed breakdown of operations provided by the CPM network is also valuable in computing progress payments. In construction work, where the job lasts for more than a brief period, provision is usually made for partial payments (e.g., monthly) to the contractor. Estimates of partial completion on which to base these progress payments are often a subject of disagreement between owner and contractor.

In a job planned by CPM, instead of broad groupings such as "concrete," "electrical work," "painting," etc., the contract is broken down into many small, well-defined operations. Since completion of each operation is usually obvious, it is not too difficult for the contractor and owner's representative to agree on which operations have been completed or on the percentage of completion for those still in progress.

To use CPM for progress payments, the estimate would be prepared on a form like that shown in Fig. 11–6, except that the amounts shown in column 3 would be an agreed schedule, rather than a budget, and would add up to the contract price. Columns 6 and 7 would be eliminated.

As each payment period nears, the Superintendent reviews the job with the owner's representative and agrees with him on the percentages to be entered in column 4. Since a specific dollar amount is associated with each operation, figuring the monthly estimate then becomes a simple clerical chore. (If the number of operations is large enough, this becomes an ideal task for a computer.) Approval of the estimate is speeded, since much of the source of argument has been reduced or eliminated.

SUMMARY

Progress control consists of checking on actual job progress, comparing it with scheduled progress, and taking the required corrective action to overcome slippages. Actual progress may be shown on the CPM network, on a modified bar chart, or on a listing of the operations.

Updating means revising the network and redoing the CPM computations to show the effects of changes and delays as well as job progress. Updating computations are similar to CPM computations, but they begin at "time now" rather than time zero, and use the time *remaining* to complete each operation instead of the original time estimates.

The detailed breakdown of operations required by CPM is easily adapted to cost control and reporting as well as to computing progress payments. Computer routines have been developed to perform some of the clerical work involved in progress reporting, updating, and cost control.

PROBLEMS

11–1. *Updating.* The network shown below (Fig. 11–9) represents a portion of a construction project that is now partially complete. The original time estimates are shown on the network.

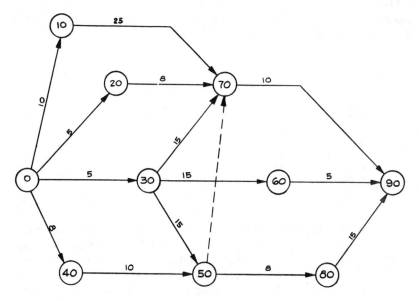

Fig. 11–9

The status of the project as of day 12 is as follows:

   a) Operations 0–10 and 0–30 have been completed.

   b) Operation 20–70 has been completed out of sequence.

   c) The following operations have been started, but require varying amounts of work left for completion:

Operation	Work Remaining (working days)
0–20	1
0–40	2
30–70	5

   d) Operation 10–70 is a delivery that is now scheduled to take
place on day 32.

   e) Because of a delay, operation 30–50 will not start until
day 14. However, the contractor now feels it can be accomplished in 10 days, instead of the 15 originally estimated.

   f) Operation 30–60 has just started today (day 12).

   g) The remaining operations have not yet been started. It is
now estimated that operation 60–90 will require 10 days
instead of the 5 originally estimated. All of the other time
estimates remain unchanged.

Update the network; determine the new completion time and critical
path. Compute float time for operations that have not yet been completed.

11–2. *Cost Analysis.* In the network of problem 11–1, the cost of each
operation was originally estimated as follows:

Operation	Estimated Cost ($)	Operation	Estimated Cost ($)
0–10	100	30–60	40
0–20	300	30–70	60
0–30	150	40–50	100
0–40	200	50–80	50
10–70	350	60–90	100
20–70	100	70–90	450
30–50	100	80–90	300
		Total	$2,400

   a) Plot a curve showing the value of scheduled work versus time.
Assume that each operation is scheduled to start at its earliest
start date, and credit each operation with its estimated cost
as of its scheduled completion date.

   b) As of day 17, the following operations have been completed,
with actual costs as shown:

Operation	Date Completed	Actual Cost ($)
0–10	10	90
0–20	13	190
0–30	5	250
0–40	14	70
20–70	8	130
30–50	17	80

Plot another curve on the same sheet showing the value of work completed by crediting each completed operation with its estimated cost as of the date it was actually finished. In terms of dollars, is the project ahead of or behind schedule?

c) Plot a third curve showing *actual* costs. (Again, credit each operation with its actual cost as of its actual completion date.) By comparing actual costs with the value of work completed, show whether the work is being accomplished efficiently. What is the amount of the cost overrun or underrun as of day 17?

12

Computer Applications

WHY COMPUTERS?

Throughout this text, we have emphasized that CPM is basically a way of thinking and planning, and that the tools required are mainly a pencil and some patience. Much of the publicity surrounding CPM has come from computer manufacturers who have naturally emphasized its association with the electronic computer. The emphasis in this text on manual methods is intended to present the other side of the case. It also reflects the belief that manual methods have a number of real advantages, some of which will be discussed in this chapter.

In spite of this, there is no question that the computer is here to stay. Competition between manufacturers is producing better, more versatile, and less expensive machines. As computers become more generally available, there will be more opportunity to use them to assist in CPM planning. Note the word "assist." The computer can take over some of the routine chores of CPM computations. It *cannot* analyze or plan a project.

In this chapter we will look at the characteristics of computers as they apply to CPM and discuss their advantages and disadvantages as compared with manual methods. In the following chapter we will review the factors to consider when selecting a computer or a program.°

° A program is a series of instructions to the computer that tells it just what computations it is to perform. See page 185.

WHAT IS A COMPUTER?

Basically, an electronic computer may be thought of as a large adding machine.* The machine can do simple arithmetical computations at fantastic speeds. The answers to these computations can be stored in the computer for use in later computations. Most important, the computer can follow a prearranged *sequence* of steps or computations under the direction of a set of instructions called a *program*. The computer also can make certain decisions that affect subsequent computations, such as: if this number is greater than that one, follow step *a;* if it is smaller, follow step *b*.

In summary, these characteristics:

Speed
Ability to store and "remember"
Ability to follow a sequence of steps
Ability to make decisions or choices

make the electronic computer a useful tool for any work involving large numbers of computations, including CPM.

THE PROGRAM

To do its job, the computer needs a program that outlines the sequence of operations that the machine must follow. Preparing a program is a tedious and expensive process, but once prepared, it can be used over and over again. A program is written for one particular computer model and cannot be used on another model, even one made by the same manufacturer. Although progress has been made in this direction, it usually requires considerable work to adapt a program from one machine to another.

---

* This discussion deals with the *digital* computer, the kind most often used for business and CPM work. There is another type of computer—the analog computer—which operates on a different principle.

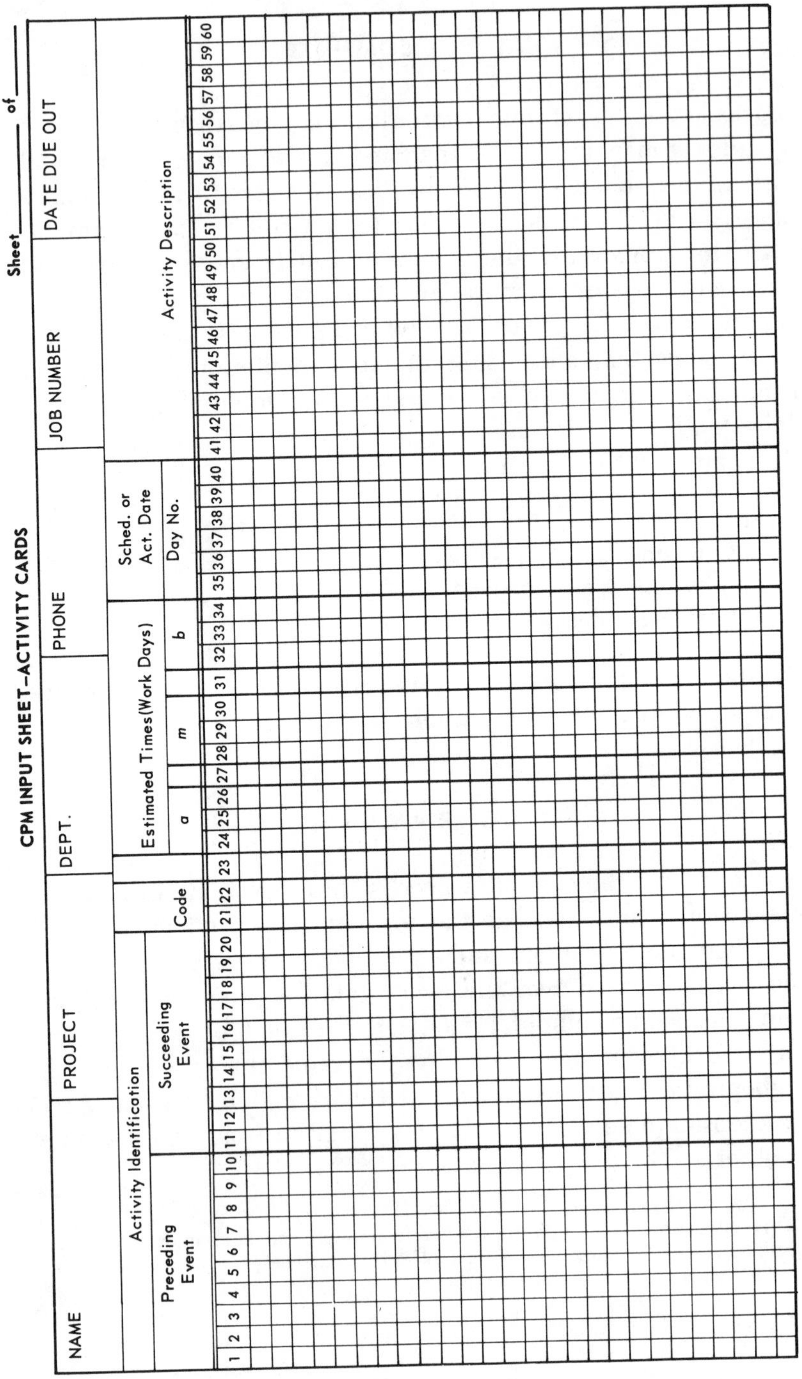

Fig. 12–1. CPM Input Sheet

INPUT

Besides the program, the machine must be fed the data for the problem at hand, called *input*. For CPM, input consists of the following information for each activity in the network:

1. The event numbers
2. The activity description
3. The estimated time (duration) for the activity

Some programs also provide for additional information, such as three time estimates (PERT), cost data, etc. These optional features will be discussed in Chapter 13.

Both the input information and the program must be in a form that the machine can understand. The most common form for input is punched cards, although punched paper tape and magnetic tape are also used. The input data are copied from the network diagram onto a form, such as Fig. 12–1. From this form or work sheet, a key-punch operator prepares the cards—one card for each line on the sheet. The cards representing the network data, together with a similar deck containing the program, are fed into the computer.

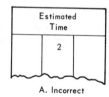
A. Incorrect

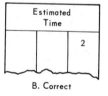
B. Correct

Fig. 12–2. Entering Data for Use in a Computer

When filling out input forms, be sure to enter each figure in the correct column; otherwise it will be misunderstood by the machine. For example, the estimated duration shown in Fig. 12–2(A) would be understood as twenty days, instead of two days.

| PROJECT: | HIGH STREET OVERPASS | | | | | | CPM | | | | 1/29/X2 |
| CONTRACTOR: | SMITH BROTHERS CONSTRUCTION COMPANY | | | | | | | | | | |

Critical	i	j	Description	Duration	ES	EF	LS	LF	TF	FF
*	1	2	Deliver Pile Rig	3	0	3	0	3		
	1	4	Procure Piles	10	0	10	15	25	1	0
*	2	3	Prepare Site	5	3	8	3	8		
*	3	6	Excav. Ftg., Bent. #2	2	8	10	8	10		
	4	5	Drive Piles, Bent. #1	3	10	13	25	28	1	0
*	6	7	Form Ftg., Bent. #2	1	10	11	10	11		
	6	11	Excav. Ftg., Bent. #3	2	10	12	25	27	1	0
*	7	8	Pour Conc. Ftg., Bent. #2	1	11	12	11	12		
*	8	9	Form Bent. #2	6	12	18	12	18		
	11	12	Form Ftg., Bent. #3	1	12	13	22	23	6	2
	5	15	Form Pile Cap, Bent. #1	1	13	14	28	29	1	

Fig. 12–3. Part of Typical CPM Output

OUTPUT

The computer prints out its results in a tabular format that looks very much like the CPM work sheet used in Chapter 5. The exact form of the *output* (as this printed tabulation is called) depends on the CPM program used. Figure 12–3 shows part of a typical CPM output.

ADVANTAGES OF COMPUTERS

Computers have certain advantages when compared with manual methods. Among these are the following:

High Speed

In most cases, the computations take just a few minutes.

Tabular Output

The computer solution provides a complete tabulation of all desired data, including float time, and can make as many copies of the output as required.

Accuracy

The computer solution is free from clerical errors (but not from errors that existed in the input data).

Least-Cost Scheduling

The computer's high speed can be used to advantage in "crashing"a project (least-cost scheduling) as described in Chapter 9. Here the manual computations become quite involved and tedious. There are, however, definite limitations on machine solutions to the least-cost scheduling problem.

Updating

The computer is valuable when the network must be updated frequently, and many copies of the revised outputs are required.

DISADVANTAGES

The preceding advantages of computers must be weighed against their limitations.

Need To Transfer Information from the Diagram

Copying the information from the diagram to the input sheet is still a manual process, and is quite subject to error. Naturally, errors in this step will result in false answers (or no answers at all).

For smaller networks it is often faster to do the computations on the network than to fill in and check the input sheet. This is particularly true when the project duration is all that is required (for example, when considering two alternate methods of doing the work). Also, there is no waiting for the computer to finish whatever other work it is doing.

Error Detection

Although the computer can recognize certain errors in network logic (such as breaks in a chain of activities), it will ignore other types of errors that would be obvious to a human being. For example, if the duration for a simple activity were entered in the wrong column, it would be understood as *sixty* days, instead of *six* days, but the machine would process it just the same.

Changes to the Network

Doing the computations often shows up the need for changes in the network diagram or the time estimates—changes that were not apparent before. Since the computer is expensive, it must be kept working and it is not feasible to have the machine stand idle while the planner restudies and adjusts his network.

With CPM, each computation is followed by a restudy of the network, and each revision to the network requires new computations. Usually, a computer's time must be fully scheduled in advance. Thus, although the initial machine computation may be very rapid, when the planner has reviewed the results and is ready for another "run"—the machine is usually busy with something else. The planner must wait his turn, which may be a matter of hours or days. With manual computations, the planner can stop at any desired point to revise his network or time estimates, and then continue the computations.

Need for Human Judgment in Planning

In spite of the speed and versatility of the computer there are a number of scheduling adjustments that can be made only by a human planner. This is especially true when "crashing" or shortening a project. The following examples will illustrate this limitation.

1. When crashing a project, the machine will select the operations in the order of their cost slopes, beginning with those with the lowest slope. Crashing one operation may involve working overtime, which may, in theory, be the cheapest way to expedite the job. As a practical matter, however, it may be necessary to work certain other entirely independent operations overtime, to avoid labor difficulties or for other reasons, with the result that the real cost of crashing this one job is much higher than the cost slope would indicate.

2. As jobs are shortened, several unrelated jobs may shift in time so that they now must be done simultaneously. This may result in competition for manpower, specialized equipment, or space. Although computer programs have been written that will schedule the work within given manpower ceilings (or other resource limitations), the machine cannot recognize when too many men are scheduled to work in a single cramped area.

3. Just as crashing one operation may increase the cost of totally unrelated operations, it may also make available "free" resources that can be used on other activities. As an example, it may be possible to expedite an operation by renting a piece of equipment, such as a crane. If the crane is needed for only a few hours (but must be rented for a full day) it can be used to expedite other operations during the remainder of that day—at practically no cost.

4. In crashing a project, the computer is limited to a mechanical shortening of the critical operations. In practice, this is not always the cheapest or best method. Careful analysis will often show that changes in the network—such as performing operations in parallel instead of in sequence—will be more effective in shortening the job, than would shortening of critical operations.

Need for Two Estimates (for Least-Cost Scheduling)

Least-cost scheduling depends on having *two* estimates for time and cost: the normal (least expensive) and the crash (shortest time). Where the computer is used for "crashing," the planner must provide these two estimates for each activity in the network, since he does not know in advance which ones will be critical. Since only a small number of the operations are usually critical, this represents considerable extra work.

Estimating time and costs for the unusual situation of all-out crash performance is a difficult job, and requires much more effort than does a "normal" estimate. The number of crash estimates should therefore be as few as possible, so that the planner can concentrate on them and give them the extra attention needed to make them accurate and useful. One way of overcoming this limitation is to make a preliminary "run" first, using either computer or manual techniques, in order to find the critical path and the float available for each operation. Crash estimates can then be limited to those activities that are now, or are likely to become, critical. For example, suppose the project must be shortened by 20 days. Crash estimates are then prepared for all critical operations and all non-critical operations whose total float is 20 days or less.

WHEN TO USE COMPUTERS

Providing the foregoing limitations are kept in mind, the high-speed electronic computer can be a useful tool. Like CPM itself, it is only a tool—not a substitute for judgment or thinking. Computers are recommended:

1. For very large projects, especially where the project cannot readily be broken down into smaller subprojects. Most authorities agree that a project of less than 100 arrows can be handled more easily manually than by machine, but there is much disagreement as to the minimum size of project that justifies computer use. It is the present author's opinion that networks of up to 200 arrows can be handled manually, and that larger projects can often be handled manually, if they can be broken down into convenient subprojects.
2. Where there is a need for frequent reports.
3. Where frequent updating is expected.
4. Where least-cost scheduling is required.

SUMMARY

Although they cannot analyze a project or prepare a network, high-speed electronic computers can be used to perform the mechanical phases of the computations quickly and accurately. And, if their limitations are kept in mind, they can be used to good effect on large, complex projects, or those where least-cost scheduling is required.

13

Selecting a Computer and a Computer Program

The preceding chapter discussed some of the advantages and disadvantages of computer solutions, as compared to manual methods. This chapter will cover the availability of computers and computer services, and outline the factors to look for when selecting a computer or a CPM program.

AVAILABILITY OF COMPUTERS

For the firm that wants to use a computer for CPM scheduling, there are several possibilities:

1. Buy or lease a computer from the manufacturer.
2. Rent time on a computer belonging to a computer service bureau or consultant.
3. Rent time on another company's computer.

Purchase or Lease

Computer manufacturers spare no pains to promote the sale or lease of their machines. Purchase or rental of a computer involves a major expense, not only for the machine, but for the space required, the host of specialized personnel—operators, programmers, etc.—and for utilities and supplies. Actually, it will

194

rarely pay for a company to buy a computer just for CPM. More often, the computer is purchased for other chores, such as accounting, payroll or scientific computations, with CPM as a useful by-product. The same reasoning applies to leasing a machine.

Computer Service Bureaus

The past few years have seen the rapid development of computer centers or service bureaus. These are commercial firms that rent out computer time to companies requiring occasional use of a computer. The machine is rented by the hour, and although the rates are high, the overall cost can be quite economical, since the user pays only for the actual computer time he requires.

Service bureaus offer several advantages:

1. Most service bureaus have skilled and experienced personnel to assist their customers in preparing the computer input.
2. Many service bureaus have available good, versatile CPM programs, which their customers may use without additional charge.
3. Once a schedule is established, the user is sure of having the machine available at the time he needs it.
4. The using company is spared not only the cost, but all the problems involved in setting up, maintaining, and operating a computer installation.

Computer centers can be found in most large cities, but lack of one in the immediate vicinity is not necessarily a drawback. If time permits, the input data can be airmailed to the computer center. Also, devices are available that transmit updating information over ordinary telephone circuits. These devices can be rented quite reasonably and, in effect, permit the user to be connected directly with a computer center in another city. Use of such devices was discussed briefly in Chapter 11 in connection with progress reporting.

In addition to the services described above, some computer centers also offer assistance in setting up the network. This type of service, which involves additional cost, really amounts to the work of a consultant.

Consultants

A number of consulting firms now offer assistance in CPM and related fields, including machine computations. An outside firm can be of help in setting up a CPM program and training company personnel. However, continued dependence on consultants is not only expensive, but it also robs the company of the improved planning and communications that can result when company personnel understand and apply CPM themselves.

Renting Time on Another Company's Computer

The number of firms with computer installations is growing daily. These include banks, manufacturing concerns, engineering firms, utilities, and others. Since this equipment is costly to own and operate, many firms are willing to rent time on their machine to outsiders. Generally, such firms furnish only the machine and its operators but no assistance to the user. For a company that understands CPM and has had some experience in preparing information for computers, this may be the most economical method, since the rates will generally be lower than those charged by a commercial computer center. Of course, the availability of the computer is subject to some uncertainty, since, reasonably enough, such firms will give priority to their own work.

SELECTING A COMPUTER AND A COMPUTER PROGRAM

Selecting a computer is closely related to the problem of finding a good CPM program, since it is the program that fixes the form of the input and determines just what information will be produced by the computer in its output. Differences between one machine and another generally relate to the speed of operation and the storage capacity (the number of letters or numbers that the machine can store or "remember" while working on a problem). Another factor is the method of feeding in the input (i.e., by means of punched cards, punched tape, etc.). These differences are not too important as far as CPM work is concerned; more important is the availability of a suitable CPM program to be used with the particular machine.

In the previous chapter we defined a computer program as a set of instructions that the machine will follow when making its computations. A large company can afford to develop a CPM program tailored to its own needs. However, most companies will prefer to make use of one of the programs already available, possibly with some minor modifications. In 1962 there were at least thirty-seven different computer programs available for CPM, PERT, or some similar network planning system. Some of the features to consider in selecting a CPM program are the following.

Availability and Cost

Programs developed by computer manufacturers are usually available free to users of their machines. A few programs are proprietary, but are offered by computer service bureaus or consultants to their customers. Other proprietary programs may be purchased or rented from the developer. One valuable source is a program library or pool featuring programs furnished by the users of a particular machine.

Size of Network

A basic consideration is the size of the network (usually the number of activities or events) that can be handled. This is determined in part by the size of the internal storage or "memory" of the computer, as well as by how efficiently this space is utilized. Machines and programs that can handle only a few hundred events are of little use, since a project of this size can usually be broken down into smaller subnetworks and handled manually. Fortunately, high-speed, large-capacity machines have made possible programs that can handle a project having thousands of activities or events.

Method of Numbering Events

Even when a computer is used, the network must still be numbered by hand—a tedious and time-consuming procedure. Some of the early CPM programs required that events be numbered *sequentially*, that is, 1, 2, 3, 4, etc. This is so undesirable as to render such programs useless, since, if any change is made in the network, it must be completely renumbered.

Other programs require that the numbers be in *ascending* order (that is, the number at the tail of the arrow must always be larger than the one at the head). This is the convention used throughout this text. The most flexible type of program will accept a network with *random* numbering (the numbers are in any order). In effect, this program renumbers the events. Note that *all* programs require that there be no *duplication* of event numbers in the network.

Speed

Except for its influence on cost, speed of operation is not · usually important with CPM, since the computations are simple, and take only a small amount of machine time.

Type of Output

Although all programs perform the same basic CPM calculations, they differ in the manner in which they present the results or output. For example, some programs furnish only earliest and latest *starting* dates but not finish dates. Some show total float and free float; others only total float. The output should be in a form that is easily understood, and the headings should have no abbreviations that will confuse the reader.

Sorting of Activities

One of the advantages of computer CPM is the ability to list (or sort) the activities in some desired order. For example, activities may be listed in order of earliest starting date, by event numbers, or by amount of float (i.e., the critical activities are listed first, followed by activities with one day of float, then all the activities with 2 days of float, etc.).

One very useful type of sort permitted by some CPM programs is a sort by *trade*. Here, each activity is given a code (letter or number) identifying the trade, subcontractor, etc. With this feature it is possible to give each subcontractor a schedule limited to his own work, and avoid the need for him to wade through many pages of data to find the activities in which he is involved.

Input Data

An easily overlooked but important factor is the type of information that the program can accept as part of the input data. Many otherwise excellent programs do not provide sufficient space for the activity descriptions, which makes it necessary to use confusing abbreviations. The program should also provide sufficient space for the event numbers. Some programs provide room for only three digits; this can be a limitation, especially if you are numbering by tens, as was recommended in Chapter 2.

Calender-Date Conversion

Like the manual CPM solution, the machine computations are figured in terms of *day numbers,* starting from some arbitrary first day (the start of contract or any other day desired). These day numbers must be converted to regular calendar dates, using a job calendar, as described in Chapter 7.

Some programs (especially PERT programs) make this conversion automatically. This is highly desirable, since it eliminates an extra manual step. However, if a program does have this feature, it is essential that it be able to adjust for holidays or other non-work days, and for the length of the work week that will be used (5 days, 6 days, etc.)

PERT Features

As discussed in Chapter 10, one of the features that distinguishes PERT is the use of three time estimates instead of one. All so-called PERT programs—and a few CPM programs—have this feature. In addition, some PERT programs compute the *variance* from which the probability of meeting a scheduled date can be determined. Some programs will also compute the probability itself, using the formulas given in Chapter 10.

Naturally, these features are important only if multiple time estimates and probabilities are required for the project. A PERT program can be used for ordinary CPM by using the same estimate of duration for the optimistic, most likely, and pessimistic time estimates.

Manpower and Resource Scheduling

Some programs can adjust the schedule in order to level out fluctuations in manpower or other resources, or to complete the job without exceeding a certain number of men in each trade. This type of scheduling is mechanical in nature and needs careful review by a human planner before being adopted as final.

Cost Computation and Least-Cost Scheduling

Certain programs include a limited cost feature (PERT/Cost) that allows tabulation of estimated costs for each activity, but does not permit use of multiple cost estimates and the determination of the most economical way of crashing the project. Computer solutions have also been developed for the problem of least-cost scheduling discussed in Chapter 9. Such a program can be a valuable time saver, especially on a large project. Limitations of these programs were discussed in the preceding chapter.

Updating

Updating was described in Chapter 11 as the process of revising the network and time estimates to show the effect of work completed and other changes. This is an important feature of any CPM program. As a minimum, the method of updating should permit you to change any of the network data easily, and to show the effect of actual completions and delays on the critical path.

Some programs provide for dropping activities from the output listing as soon as they are completed. Thus, the report becomes shorter each time, and attention is focused on the work still remaining for completion.

Error Checking

One important feature of a good CPM program is the ability to spot certain types of errors in the input data. The computer should be able to verify:

1. That there is at least one continuous path through the network with no breaks.
2. That there are no "dangling" events. This means that all events except the final event have at least one event following, and all events except the starting event have at least one preceding event.
3. That there are no loops in the network.
4. That the same event number does not appear twice in the network.

If any of the above conditions exists, the program should print out a code that tells the type of error and locates it by the event numbers involved.

Summarizing and Condensing Networks

Some programs have a special feature that permits them to summarize and condense a series of subnetworks into an overall network. This can be useful in dealing with large, complex projects.

Other Special Features

There are many other special features offered by specific programs. A few examples are:

1. *Scheduling Float.* At least one program will schedule float, allocating it among the activities in accordance with an importance code that the user has previously designated.
2. *Multiple Start and Finish.* Although most programs are limited to the standard single starting event and single ending event, some are able to accept multiple starting and/or ending events.
3. *Graphical Outputs.* Some programs will produce graphical displays, such as a bar chart. However, no program is presently available that will mechanically produce the CPM network.

COST OF COMPUTER SERVICES

A typical cost for computer time at a large service bureau is $150 per hour. This includes use of the firm's CPM program and the necessary forms and materials. A typical project involving several hundred activities required about one-half hour of computer time, including least-cost scheduling calculations. Simple CPM required only a few minutes of machine time.

In addition to the machine time, there is the cost of preparing the computer input. Usually, the input data must be key-punched into cards or tape with one card required for each activity. Key-punching costs from $5 to $6 per hour, and a skilled operator can turn out several hundred cards per hour. Key-punching is a significant factor only when setting up the project. For updating, new cards are required only for those few activities in which changes have taken place.

Some computer centers have a special rate for CPM work, based on the number of activities (arrows) in the network. Typical prices are 20¢ to 35¢ per activity, depending on the size of the network, with key-punching extra. This type of charge permits the user to figure his costs in advance, but is usually more costly than the hourly charge.

SUMMARY

Purchase or lease of a computer is rarely advisable for CPM work alone. Computer time may be rented from service bureaus or companies that own their own machines. Selection of a computer program should consider the restrictions on the form of the network such as size and event numbering, the types of output available, and desired special features, such as calendar conversion, least-cost scheduling, or PERT computations. Provision for periodic updating and for some internal error checking is essential.

14

Implementing the CPM Program

The extent of use of CPM varies widely. Some firms use only the network diagram as a means of "seeing" the job more clearly. Others perform the computations, but do so only to determine the completion time. Still others make use of some or all of the techniques of planning, scheduling, expediting, and project control that we have described in this text. In this chapter, we will attempt to suggest how CPM might be implemented by a construction firm. In doing so, we will bring together the various steps that have been previously discussed in separate chapters. In addition, this chapter will suggest procedures for introducing CPM into a firm. Listing of suggested steps for implementing CPM does not imply a rigid procedure. Rather, each company should select those ideas that meet its own needs.

STEPS IN USING CPM

Use of CPM by a contracting firm might follow a cycle such as this:

Preliminary Network

When bidding on a contract, if time permits, a rough network should be prepared containing about 100 activities for a project of average complexity. Many specifications now require a preliminary network of this type to accompany the bid. However, even if not required, it can serve as a valuable aid in estimating, as follows:

1. As a check on the overall project duration.
2. To assist the estimators and others working on the job in visualizing the construction sequence.
3. To spot potential trouble spots and missed operations.
4. To make a rough check on overall manpower levels.

Project Planning

When the contractor is awarded the job, preparation of a detailed CPM network should be a part of the preliminary job planning. The rough network prepared during the bidding stage is now expanded into a detailed arrow diagram.

Sufficient time must be allotted for this, since the success of the planning depends on the care that goes into the preparation of the network. Also, it is essential that those responsible for accomplishment of the project (including major subcontractors) participate in preparing the diagram. On the other hand, experience has shown that it is not practical for more than a few people (say five) to work on one diagram at a time.

The recommended procedure is to have a team consisting of the project manager and his field superintendents prepare the network with the assistance of one or two of the major subcontractors. These diagrams are then reviewed by the other subcontractors and revised as necessary. Additional comments on practical aspects of the network diagramming step are included later in this chapter.

Estimating Times

The initial diagram shows all operations, including those of subcontractors, and all actions by the owner and architect on which the contractor depends, such as approvals, color selections, etc. Following its completion, times are estimated for as many operations as possible. At this stage, subcontractors who have not participated in drawing up the network should be called in, singly or in small groups, to review it and to estimate the times for their operations.

Subcontractors who are not familiar with CPM scheduling can usually be indoctrinated in a few minutes with the help of the arrow diagram. Once they understand the system, the subcontractors will frequently be able to point out flaws in the "logic" (the sequence of operations) of the diagram as it applies to their work. Unless the subcontractors have been thoroughly trained in CPM, it is much better to present them with some kind of network that they can review and criticize, rather than to explain the "rules" and ask them to prepare one from scratch. Minor subcontractors and material suppliers can furnish time estimates by telephone.

CPM Computations

After review by subcontractors and entering of time estimates, CPM computations are made and the critical path identified (Chapters 5 and 6).

Review

This first CPM schedule should now be reviewed and any of the techniques described in Chapters 7, 8, and 9, such as shortening, manpower scheduling, resource trade-offs, or least-cost scheduling, applied as desired. As a minimum, it is recommended that the operations on the critical path and those with little float time (near-critical) be reviewed. Since these operations now control the project duration, more intensive study is usually justified. It may be found that the time estimates were unrealistic, or that the sequence of operations was not correct. Necessary adjustments should be made.

Scheduling

The process of review and revision should be continued until a reasonably satisfactory schedule is obtained. Further refinement aimed at achieving a "perfect" schedule is not justified. At this point, detailed work schedules are prepared. It is important to schedule the non-critical activities as well as the critical ones, in order properly to allocate float and avoid confusion. The schedule may be shown directly on the arrow diagram, or on a listing of the operations. Copies are made and distributed to field superintendents, purchasing agents, subcontractors, and others concerned. At this time, the diagram is usually redrawn in neater and more legible form.

If a subcontractor plays only a minor role in the project, it is better to abstract for him the starting and completion dates for his operations, rather than to expect him to pick his own operations out of a complete schedule. If electronic computers are available, they can often be programmed to print out separate schedules for each trade. This is done by assigning each major trade or subcontractor a code number, which is used along with the operation description in the computer input.

Project Management and Control

The completed network and resulting schedule are used by the project manager and superintendents to control the job. As the work proceeds, actual job progress is noted on the charts or schedules as described in Chapter 11.

Summary reports are submitted at periodic intervals, usually weekly, biweekly, or monthly. These will report project-completion status and may also include costs. Corrective action is taken when necessary to bring the job back to schedule.

Updating

If changes are extensive, the network is periodically revised and updated and computations are redone to show the effect of changes or delays and to determine new completion dates.

HINTS ON NETWORK DIAGRAMMING

The rules for drawing CPM networks were presented in Chapter 2. Here we want to add a few suggestions, based more on practical experience than on CPM theory.

In drawing networks for large projects, do not try to show the entire project on a single chart. It is usually better to break down the project into its main parts, and use a separate chart for each part. This permits several teams to work at once, and also provides a chart that is more easily read and grasped. The National Aeronautics and Space Agency (NASA) requires its contractors to submit their network charts on 21-inch by 48-inch sheets, with approximately 250 arrows on each sheet. This is good practice for most CPM work.

Events that show the relationship between different phases of the work and that appear on more than one sheet are called "interface" events. These may be shown by means of special symbols, as in Fig. 14–1. These special symbols may also be

Fig. 14–1.   Interface Events

used on a single sheet in order to avoid lines criss-crossing from one part to another; this use should be kept to a minimum, however.

When doing the computations (and particularly when using electronic computers), one must avoid either omitting the interface activities or including them twice.

INTRODUCING CPM TO YOUR COMPANY

The reception of Critical Path Method, PERT, and related scheduling methods by industry has ranged from wild enthusiasm to outright rejection. Not all companies have met with equal success in their attempts to use CPM. The experiences of many companies, as expressed in letters to the editors of technical publications, comments at meetings, and informal discussions, point up the fact that success or failure often depends on how the system was introduced into the company.

The following paragraphs suggest procedures that successful users of CPM have found beneficial, and will point out some of the errors and pitfalls that have plagued its acceptance by others.

SOME DO'S

If the company's use of CPM is to be successful, the following points are essential.

Obtain Management Support

The first requirement is that company management give wholehearted support to the use of network scheduling methods and make their feeling known "down the line" to operating personnel. Otherwise, personnel will not put forth the extra thought and effort required to make CPM a success.

Plan for Introduction of CPM and Provide Necessary Resources

Introducing CPM requires training of personnel and may involve changes in company procedures. Thorough planning is essential if its use is to be successful. Planning must consider just how CPM will affect each of the firm's operations. Management must also be willing to devote the necessary time, manpower, and other resources required.

Make Use of Line Supervisors

Some companies delegate CPM planning to a special CPM staff or individual. Although specialists may be helpful with the mechanics of the system, it is essential that line supervisors be directly involved in the planning and scheduling process in order that the planning be realistic.

Provide Adequate Training

Training should be of two types: For project managers, estimators, project engineers, and supervisors who will be using CPM in their daily work, and who must be familiar with the computations, formal training is a must. This should include problems as well as lectures, since it is only by working examples that personnel acquire the necessary confidence and know-how.

For top management and other personnel who require a familiarity with CPM, but not a knowledge of its mechanics, introductory lectures on the principles and applications of CPM are satisfactory.

SOME PROBLEMS TO BE EXPECTED

The following are a few of the problems that have been found to impede the acceptance and implementation of CPM:

Resistance to Change

One problem is the human tendency to resist change and new methods. It is the author's feeling, however, that if properly presented, the principles of CPM can be understood and accepted by most persons. There is something straightforward and logical about CPM that makes it easily grasped even by non-technical people. Adequate support by management, coupled with proper training, will go a long way toward obtaining confidence and cooperation.

Some companies find that certain personnel, particularly at the foreman level, will not participate effectively in CPM planning, regardless of training. In this case it is best to avoid the use of CPM at the lowest supervisory levels, but to translate its results into simpler charts or schedules with which the foremen are familiar.

Improper Preparation of Network

Throughout this text, we have emphasized the importance of the thinking and analysis that go into the CPM network. Laziness in preparing the network always leads to inaccurate or meaningless results. A common error in network planning is to consider only the execution phase of the project (such as field work, in the case of a construction project). If the network is to be of value, it must reflect all necessary operations: design, procurement, shop drawings, etc., including those operations not under the contractor's control, such as owner approvals.

Unrealistic Time Estimates

A natural tendency is to think in terms of scheduled dates, rather than to estimate times for each operation independently. Proper training of personnel is essential to overcome this tendency. For CPM to be effective, durations must be as realistic as possible. This may seem to conflict with the rule given previously that no restrictions on manpower should be assumed when preparing the initial network. However, after the computations are done and the critical path is identified, critical and near-critical activities should be carefully restudied and time estimates adjusted to reflect competition for men, space, and equipment.

Lack of Follow-Up

If CPM is to be more than just a planning tool, it is essential to follow up and insure that activities are completed on schedule and that positive action is taken to restore and correct slippages. Activities on non-critical paths cannot be allowed to slip to the extent that their total float is exceeded, nor can the same total float be used by more than one activity. Finally, the schedule must be updated to reflect the effects of delays and changes in plan.

SUMMARY

The steps in implementing CPM make use of techniques covered in previous chapters. They include:

1. Preliminary network as an aid in bidding.
2. Detailed network.
3. Obtaining time estimates.
4. Locating the critical path.
5. Review and adjustment of the network.
6. Preparation of the final project schedule.
7. Use of the schedule to control and monitor the work.

Subcontractors as well as those charged with project execution should participate in the planning process.

In introducing CPM into a department or a company, it is important to plan carefully for its use, to obtain the full support of management, to utilize line supervisors, and to provide adequate training for those who will use the technique. Problems in acceptance of CPM often stem from human resistance to change, but may also be caused by carelessness in preparing the network or failure to follow up during the accomplishment of the project.

CPM can be a valuable management tool if given adequate support and if its introduction and use are given the required thought and effort.

PROBLEMS

14–1. *CPM As a Contract Requirement.* You are a general contractor who has just been awarded a contract for construction of a building. The owner requires the use of CPM scheduling. The time schedule is tight and there is a penalty (liquidated damages) for late completion. You want to make sure that each subcontractor will cooperate in the CPM scheduling. In addition, you want each subcontractor to complete his operations within the scheduled time, and not delay other trades.

Prepare an outline of a contract clause to be included in all subcontracts that will cover these requirements.

Bibliography

In the short time since their development, many hundreds of articles, brochures, studies, and books have been published on CPM, PERT, and related methods. The following list includes only those that will be of general use to the student or that present one particular facet of the subject not covered elsewhere. For a complete bibliography the reader is referred to:

FRY, B. L. *Network-Type Management Control System Bibliography,* Memorandum RM-3074-PR, The RAND Corporation, Santa Monica, Calif., 1963.

BOOKS AND PAMPHLETS

CHRISTENSEN, BORGE M. *Critical Path Method—An Optimizing Time-Cost Planning and Scheduling Method,* published as Brochure No. CPB-184 under the title: *GE 225 and CPM for Precise Project Planning.* Phoenix, Ariz.: General Electric Computer Department, 1961.

————. *Network Models for Project Scheduling.* Brochure CPB-221 (reprinted from *Machine Design,* May 10 to July 19, 1962), Phoenix, Ariz.: General Electric Computer Department.

CPM in Construction, A Manual for General Contractors. Washington, D.C.: The Associated General Contractors of America, 1965.

DOD and NASA Guide: PERT COST. Washington 25, D.C.: Department of Defense, Office of the Secretary, and National Aeronautics and Space Agency, 1962.

FONDAHL, JOHN W. *A Non-Computer Approach to the Critical Path Method for the Construction Industry* (2d ed). Stanford, Calif.: Department of Civil Engineering, Stanford University, 1962.

General Information Manual: PERT . . . A Dynamic Project Planning and Control Method. Publication No. E 20-8067-1, White Plains, N.Y.: International Business Machines Corp., Data Processing Division (undated).

LATTERNER, C. G., DRESDNER, D. M., SPIECH, J. A., and USLAN, G. M. *A Programmed Introduction to PERT.* New York: John Wiley & Sons, Inc., 1963.

MacKENZIE, D. E., HICKEY, A. E., and AUTOR, S. M. *Programmed Instruc-*

tion in PERT/CPM (Instruction Kit). Newburyport, Mass.: Entelek, Inc., 1963.

A *Manual for Applying the Critical Path Method to Highway Department Engineering and Administration.* E. S. Preston & Associates, Ltd., Washington, D.C., 1963.

MARTINO, R. L. *Project Management and Control.* Vol. I: *Finding the Critical Path.* New York: American Management Association, 1963.

————. *Project Management and Control.* Vol. II: *Applied Operational Planning.* New York: American Management Association, 1964.

————. *Project Management and Control.* Vol. III: *Allocating and Scheduling Resources.* New York: American Management Association, 1965.

PERT Instruction Manual and System and Procedures for The Program Evaluation System. Washington, D.C.: Special Projects Office, Bureau of Naval Weapons, Department of the Navy, U.S. Government Printing Office, 1960.

PHILIPS, CECIL R., and MODER, JOSEPH J. *Manual of Critical Path Theory and Practice.* Atlanta, Ga.: Management Science Atlanta, Inc., 1962.

————. *Catalog of Computer Programs for PERT and Similar Management Systems.* Technical Paper No. 13, Silver Springs, Md.: Operations Research, Inc., 1962.

SHAFFER, L. R., RITTER, J. B., and MEYER, W. L. *Introduction to the Critical Path Method.* Urbana, Ill.: University of Illinois, 1963.

STIRES, DAVID M., and MURPHY, MAURICE M. *PERT and CPM.* Boston, Massachusetts: Materials Management Institute, 1962.

The Story of the Critical Path Method (booklet containing reprints of articles from *Engineering News-Record*). New York: McGraw-Hill Publishing Co., Inc., 1963.

WALDRON, A. JAMES. *Fundamentals of Project Planning and Control.* Haddonfield, N.J.: A. James Waldron, 1963.

ARTICLES AND PAPERS

ALLEN, LARRY N. "Implementing CPM with Cost Monitoring for Multitype Projects," Technical Paper No. 65-C.2, presented at 9th National Meeting of the American Association of Cost Engineers (June–July, 1965).

ARAS, RESTAN M., and SURKIS, JULIUS. "PERT and CPM Techniques in Project Management," *Journal of the Construction Division, Proceedings of the American Society of Civil Engineers,* XC, No. CO 1, Proc. Paper 3823 (March, 1964), 1–25.

BEUTEL, MORRIS L. "Computer Estimates Costs, Saves Time, Money," *Engineering News-Record* (February 28, 1963), 26.

BOVERIE, RICHARD T. "The Practicalities of PERT," *IEEE Transactions on Engineering Management* (March, 1963), 3–5.

COST CONTROL COMMITTEE, METROPOLITAN NEW YORK SECTION, AMERICAN ASSOCIATION OF COST ENGINEERS. "Can the Application of the Critical Path Method Assist Cost Control?" Technical Paper No. 63-25 (May, 1963).

————. "CPM Five Years After—An Appraisal," Technical Paper No. 65-C.7, presented at 9th National Meeting of the American Association of Cost Engineers (June–July, 1965).

GALBREATH, ROBERT V. "Computer Program for Leveling Resource Usage," *Journal of the Construction Division, Proceedings of the American Society of Civil Engineers,* XCI, No. CO 1, Proc. Paper 4327 (May, 1965), 107–24.

GEOGHAN, W. C. "Resource Allocation and Critical Path Techniques," Technical Paper No. 65-C.3, presented at 9th National Meeting of the American Association of Cost Engineers (June–July, 1965).

GLEASON, WILLIAM J., JR., and RANIERI, JOSEPH J. "First Five Years of the Critical Path Method," *Journal of the Construction Division, Proceedings of the American Society of Civil Engineers,* XC, No. CO 1, Proc. Paper 3832 (March, 1964), 27–36.

HOWARD, BURL W. "CPM—As Complete Project Management," *Journal of the Construction Division, Proceedings of the American Society of Civil Engineers,* XCI, No. CO 1, Proc. Paper 4324 (May, 1965), 99–106.

JONAS, D. L. "Seattle Viaduct Redesigned Using CPM," *Civil Engineering* (October, 1964), 46–47.

KEANE, JOHN A., and TRAWICK, JACK D. "Manpower by Critical Path Method," *Civil Engineering* (July, 1964), 42–43.

MODER, JOSEPH J. "How to do CPM Scheduling without a Computer," *Engineering News-Record* (March 14, 1963), 30–36.

MONAHAN, JOHN O. "The Critical Path Method—How To Use It," *Construction Methods* (May, 1962), 130–35.

O'BRIEN, JAMES J. "CPM in Electrical Construction," *Electrical Construction and Maintenance* (January, 1964), 70–73.

PETERSON, R. J. "CPM Helps an A-E Consultant Schedule Engineering Manpower," *Engineering News-Record* (June 27, 1963), 22–25.

PHILLIPS, CECIL R. "Fifteen Key Features of Computer Programs for CPM and PERT," *Journal of Industrial Engineering,* XV, No. 1 (January–February, 1964), 14–20.

SAMPSELL, DAVID F. "A Graphical PERT Analog," *The Military Engineer,* No. 367 (September–October, 1963), 321.

SANDO, FRANCIS A. "CPM—What Factors Determine Its Success?" *Architectural Record* (April, 1964), 210–16; (May, 1964), 202–4.

SMITH, KENNETH F. "PERT-Cost Revisited, What Is the Value of Value?" *Navy Management Review,* X, No. 8 (August, 1965), 4–8.

VAN KRUGEL, E. "Introduction to CPM," *Architectural Record* (September, 1964), 337–44.

VOGELER, ROBERT B. "Critical Path Scheduling—Philosophy and Experience," Technical Paper No. 51, presented at the 6th Annual Convention of the American Association of Cost Engineers (June, 1962).

WHITE, GLENN L. "New Approach to CPM Gives Prompt Solutions to Difficult Problems," *The Constructor* (May, 1964), 27–29.

ZAHLER, CHARLES W. "Use of Critical Path Techniques," *Journal of the Structural Division, Proceedings of the American Society of Civil Engineers,* LXXXIX, No. ST 4, Proc. Paper 3589 (August, 1963).

Glossary

Activity. An individual element of a project, having a definite beginning and a definite end. An activity always requires a certain amount of time for its accomplishment, and usually requires some kind of resources.

Activity-Oriented Network. A network that emphasizes the activities, rather than the events.

Algorithm. A computational routine for solving a mathematical problem.

All-Crash. A schedule under which all operations in the project are "crashed," that is, performed in the shortest possible time.

Arrow. A directed line used to show the accomplishment of an operation in the network (arrow) diagram. In most CPM work the length of the arrow has no significance.

Arrow Diagram. A graph showing the sequence and dependencies between the elements of the project. As used in this text, same as network diagram.

Arrow Notation. A form of network diagram used in CPM in which the activities are shown by *arrows* and the events by the intersections of the arrows (usually shown as circles).

Base Line. In arrow diagramming, a vertical line used to enlarge an event bubble when there are many activity arrows entering or leaving it. Frequently used instead of a circle for the starting or ending event.

Bell Curve. So called because of its characteristic, bell-like shape. *See also* Normal Distribution.

Bubble. *See* Node.

Circle-Line Notation. A form of network diagram in which the operations are shown by *circles* and the relationship or dependencies between the operations are shown by lines drawn between the circles.

Computer Program. A set of instructions written in a code that is understood by the computer. The program tells the computer what operations to perform and in what sequence.

Cost Slope. The slope of the time-cost curve for an operation. For most cases:

$$\text{Cost Slope} = \frac{\text{Crash Cost} - \text{Normal Cost}}{\text{Normal Duration} - \text{Crash Duration}}$$

Crash Cost. The minimum direct cost required to complete the operation (or project) in the least possible time (the crash time).

Crash Point. The point on a time-cost curve marking the intersection of the *crash cost* and *crash duration*.

Crash Time. (Duration): The shortest time in which it is possible to complete the operation or project, regardless of cost.

Crashing. (1) Shortening an operation by adding additional resources. (2) Shortening a project by shortening the critical operations in such a manner that each resulting schedule is the most economical one possible at that duration. *See* Least-Cost Scheduling.

Critical Operation. An operation whose duration cannot be increased without increasing completion time of the overall project.

Critical Path. The chain of operations in the network having the longest total duration. The durations of these activities determine the project duration.

Dependency. A relationship between activities such that one cannot start until the other is finished.

Deterministic. An approach to project planning in which it is assumed that the durations of the activities can be known or determined; characteristic of most CPM planning; opposed to *probabilistic* in which the opposite is assumed.

Deviation (z). In PERT, the difference between the *Scheduled Event Time* (T_S) and the *Earliest Event Time* (T_E), expressed in terms of the standard deviation (σ)

$$z = \frac{T_S - T_E}{\sigma_{T_E}}$$

Used in probability tables to find the probability of meeting a scheduled date.

Digital Computer. A high-speed calculating machine in which information is handled in discrete elements (digits). The abacus and the electric adding machine are examples of elementary digital computers.

Direct Costs. As used in this text, those costs of accomplishing an operation that are directly related to the time in which the operation is completed.

Dragout. An increase in the time for accomplishing an operation, resulting in an unwanted increase in cost; e.g., when the size of the work crew is reduced to below the minimum needed to work efficiently.

Dummy or Dummy Arrow. A fictitious activity, requiring zero time and no resources for its accomplishment, used to show proper network relationships. Dummies are usually shown by dotted lines on the arrow diagram.

Duration. An estimate of how long an operation will take in hours, days, working days, or other time units.

Early Finish. The day an operation will be completed if it is started at its early start time. This is the earliest date on which the operation can be finished.

Early Start. The day preceding the first day an operation can begin.

Event. A point in time that marks the start or completion of one or more operations. Events do not require time or resources.

Event-Oriented Network. A network that emphasizes the events rather than the activities.

Expected Time (t_e). In PERT, the expected time is the weighted average of the *optimistic, most likely,* and *pessimistic* times for an activity:

$$t_e = \frac{a + 4m + b}{6}$$

Float Time. A measure of the leeway available in completing an operation. Various kinds of float measure how much the operation can be delayed without affecting other operations, total project completion time, etc. *See also* Total Float, Free Float, Interfering Float.

Free Float. The amount of time an operation may be delayed without affecting *any* following operations.

Frequency Distribution. In probability, this is a graph showing the variation in magnitude of some factor compared to the number of times (frequency) that magnitude would be expected to occur. For example, a frequency distribution for men's heights might show the number (or percentage) of men who might be expected to have various heights.

Indirect Costs. As used in this text, those costs that do not vary with the time for completing an individual operation but that generally are related to the completion time for the overall project.

Input. Information prepared for use with an electronic computer.

Interface. (1) An event or activity that appears twice in a CPM diagram, either twice on the same sheet or on two sheets. This is done for convenience. (2) An event or activity that connects and relates two different phases of the same project.

Interfering Float. The difference between *total float* and *free float* for any operation. Use of the interfering float does affect subsequent operations.

Job Calendar. A calendar that converts from day numbers to calendar dates.

Latest Finish. The day on which the operation must be completed if the overall project is not to be delayed.

Latest Start Time. The last day on which the operation can begin without delaying the project completion time.

Lead Time. A loose term used to describe the time that elapses between the making of a decision and its physical result. For example, in material deliveries, the lead time is the time elapsed from the moment it is decided to order the materials to the time they arrive. It may include the time for preparing specifications, taking bids, awarding contracts, fabricating, and shipping. Sometimes, lead time is used to denote the time for fabricating and shipping only.

Least-Cost Scheduling. The process of shortening a project step by step, in such a manner that each resulting schedule represents the cheapest possible way to complete the job in that particular time. *See* Crashing.

Logic. In CPM, the relationships and dependencies among the activities that make up a project, as shown by the arrow diagram; the planned sequence of work.

Loop. A logical error in a network diagram: *a* depends on *b; b* depends on *c;* and *c* depends on *a*.

Management by Exception. A technique of management under which the manager takes action only when performance fails to meet predetermined limits or standards.

Manpower Curve. A graph that shows the variation in the number of men required over the life of the project.

Manpower Leveling. Adjusting the schedule and manpower assignments to reduce manpower fluctuations over the life of the job.

Milestone. An important event in a project, such as completion of a major component or phase.

Most Likely Time (m). In PERT, this is the estimator's opinion of the most likely time for completion of the activity. This is what he would give if he were asked for only one time estimate.

Network. *See* Arrow Diagram.

Node. Technical name for the junction between arrows in the arrow diagram. In the most common CPM nomenclature, nodes represent *events* (points in time) and are shown by circles.

Normal Cost. The cost of doing the work in the most efficient way, without regard to how long it takes.

Normal Distribution. A frequency distribution curve with a characteristic bell shape that describes many natural processes of a random nature.

Normal Point. The point on a time-cost graph formed by the intersection of the *normal time* and *normal cost*.

Normal Time (Duration). The time to complete the operation or project at lowest (normal) cost.

Operation. Any element of a project having a definite beginning and end and requiring time for completion; as used in this book, same as Activity.

Optimistic Time (a). In PERT, the shortest time in which the activity could be completed if everything goes exceptionally well. The activity has only one chance in a hundred of being completed within the optimistic time.

Optimum Schedule (Duration). That schedule resulting in the smallest *total* project cost.

Output. The calculations or tabulations produced by a computer.

PERT (Program Evaluation and Review Technique). A project planning and reporting technique that makes use of the network diagram, and uses a probabilistic approach to determining operation durations.

Pessimistic Time (b)**.** In PERT, the longest time that the activity could possibly take (barring acts of God), if everything goes badly. The activity might be expected to exceed this time only once in a hundred times.

Planning. The process of analyzing a project in order to break it down into its elements (operations) and of determining the logical order in which the operations must be performed.

Probabilistic. An approach to project planning that assumes that the durations of the activities cannot be known with any degree of certainty, but can be approached statistically in terms of probabilities; characteristic of most PERT planning; opposed to *deterministic*.

Progress Control. The process of determining the status of completion of the project with relation to the selected schedule, and taking corrective action where required to overcome delays and slippages.

Progress Payments. In construction work, payments made to the contractor (usually monthly) on account of work completed to date. Also called *partial payments*.

Project. An undertaking having a definite goal or object and consisting of a number of individual elements or operations that must be completed in some sequence to achieve the goal. A project must always have a definite beginning and a definite end.

Resource Allocation. Assigning men, machines, etc., to each operation in the project.

Resource Leveling. Assignment of actual starting dates and allocation of resources in such a manner as to minimize fluctuations in the amount of any one resource required on the project. *See also* Manpower Leveling.

Resources. That which is required to accomplish an operation—manpower, money, materials, equipment, space, etc. Some texts on CPM also consider *time* a resource.

Scheduled Date (T_S)**.** A specified target date to which the project must conform.

Scheduling. Assigning actual calendar dates to each element or operation of a project.

Simulation. Testing a proposed course of action by means of a mathematical model.

Slack Time. A measure of leeway or delay allowable. As used in this text, slack time is associated with an *event*, and is the difference between the earliest expected date (T_E) and the latest allowable date (T_L). Slack time measures how much the event can be delayed without delaying the final project completion.

$$\text{Slack Time} = T_E - T_L$$

Slippage. Delay in accomplishing one or more operations.

Standard Deviation (σ) (Sigma). A statistical measure of the degree of uncertainty associated with an estimate. In PERT, it is used to measure the "spread" of the time estimates. For any activity:

$$\sigma = \frac{b - a}{6}$$

The standard deviation for an event time (T_E) is found by taking the square root of the *variance* associated with that event:

$$\sigma_{T_E} = \sqrt{V}$$

Stretch-Out. Deliberately increasing the time for accomplishing a non-critical operation by reducing the resources allocated to it, to effect an overall cost saving.

Time-Cost Curve. A graph showing the relation between the time for completion (duration) of the operation (or project) and the cost to complete it at that duration. Used in *Least-Cost Scheduling*.

Total (Project) Cost. The sum of the *direct* and the *indirect costs*.

Total Float. The amount of time an operation may be delayed without affecting the duration of the project.

Trade-Off. An exchange of resources, such as men, money, or equipment, between operations in order to achieve some goal such as faster completion. Also used to describe an exchange between additional resources (i.e., money) and time.

Updating. Making changes in the CPM network diagram and/or time estimates to show the effect of changed conditions such as completed activities, delays, changes in plan, etc.

Variance (v) and (V). A statistical term equal to the square of the *standard deviation* (σ):

$$v = \sigma^2$$

For an event time, the variance (V) is found by adding the variances along the longest path leading to that event.

Solutions to Problems

CHAPTER 2

2–1.

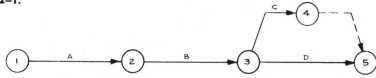

2–2.

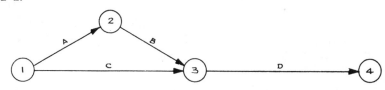

2–3.

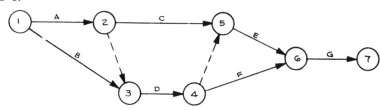

2–4.

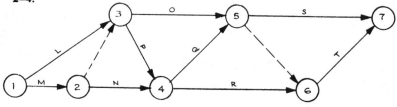

2–5.

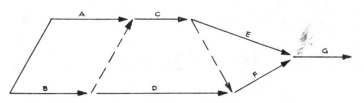

2–6.

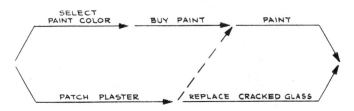

The above solution results from the (arbitrary) condition that Jack will not replace the glass until after he has patched the plaster. If this restriction is removed, the solution is as follows:

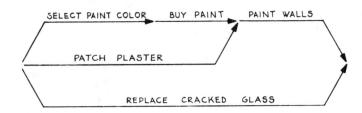

2–7.

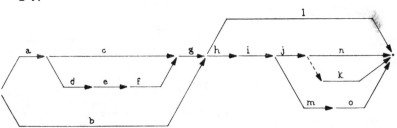

Solution assumes that spare tire and tools are kept in the trunk in such a way that one may be removed without disturbing the other.

CHAPTER 3

3–1.

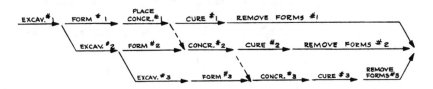

3–2.

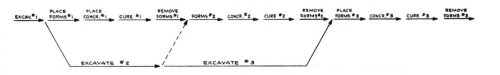

CHAPTER 4

4–1.

Job (1)	Total Man-Hours (2)	Man-Days (2) ÷ 8 (3)	Crew Size (4)	Total Days (3) ÷ (4) (5)	Wall Section (6)	Duration (days)	
						Theo-retical	Use for CPM *
						(7)	
Excavation	144	18	3	6	#1	2	2
					#2	2	2
					#3	2	2
Erect forms	80	10	2	5	#1	1⅔	2
					#2	1⅔	2
					#3	1⅔	2
Mix and place concrete	72	9	6	1½	#1	½	1
					#2	½	1
					#3	½	1
Remove forms	16	2	2	1	#1	⅓	1
					#2	⅓	1
					#3	⅓	1

* Durations of less than 1 working day are shown as 1 day.

4–1. (*Cont.*)

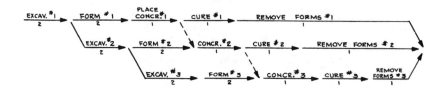

CHAPTER 5

5–1.

Node Numbers		Description	Dura-tion	Earliest		Latest		Float	
i	j			Start	Finish	Start	Finish	Total	Free
1	2		2	0	2	1	3	1	0
1	3		5	0	5	0	5	0	_*
2	4		5	2	7	3	8	1	1
3	4		3	5	8	5	8	0	_*
4	5		9	8	17	8	17	0	_*
4	6		2	8	10	16	18	8	7
5	6		0	17	17	18	18	1	0
5	7		7	17	24	17	24	0	_*
6	7		6	17	23	18	24	1	1
7	8		2	24	26	24	26	0	_*

*Critical.

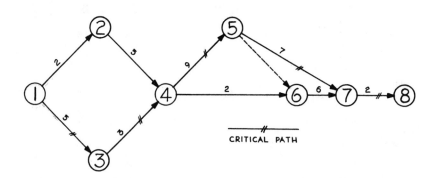

CRITICAL PATH

5–2.

Node Numbers		Description	Dura-tion	Earliest		Latest		Float	
i	j			Start	Finish	Start	Finish	Total	Free
1	3	A	8	0	8	0	8	0	—*
1	7	G	12	0	12	160	·172	160	0
1	9	B	8	0	8	164	172	164	4
3	5	C	160	8	168	8	168	0	—*
3	11	D	120	8	128	88	208	80	80
3	17	F	16	8	24	216	232	208	208
3	23	E	16	8	24	248	264	240	240
5	11	J	40	168	208	168	208	0	—*
7	9	Dummy	0	12	12	172	172	160	0
9	11	H	36	12	48	172	208	160	160
11	15	K	24	208	232	208	232	0	—*
15	17	Dummy	0	232	232	232	232	0	—*
15	19	M	8	232	240	248	256	16	0
17	21	L	24	232	256	232	256	0	—*
19	21	Dummy	0	240	240	256	256	16	16
19	27	Q	4	240	244	280	284	40	40
21	23	N	8	256	264	256	264	0	—*
23	25	O	16	264	280	264	280	0	—*
25	27	P	4	280	284	280	284	0	—*

*Critical operation.

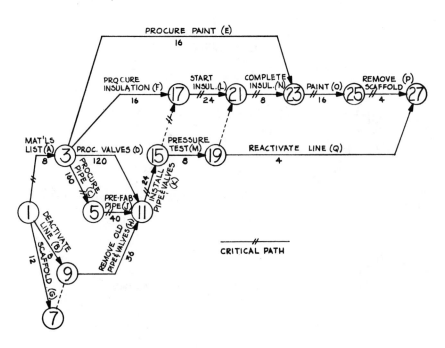

5–3.

| Node Numbers | | | Dura-tion | Earliest | | Latest | | Float | |
i	j	Description		Start	Finish	Start	Finish	Total	Free
1	3	Excavate #1	2	0	2	0	2	0	—*
3	5	Erect Forms #1	2	2	4	4	6	2	0
3	11	Excavate #2	2	2	4	2	4	0	—*
5	7	Place Concrete #1	1	4	5	6	7	2	0
7	9	Cure Concrete #1	1	5	6	9	10	4	0
7	13	Dummy	0	5	5	7	7	2	1
9	27	Remove Forms #1	1	6	7	10	11	4	4
11	13	Erect Forms #2	2	4	6	5	7	1	0
11	19	Excavate #3	2	4	6	4	6	0	—*
13	15	Place Concrete #2	1	6	7	7	8	1	0
15	17	Cure Concrete #2	1	7	8	9	10	2	0
15	21	Dummy	0	7	7	8	8	1	1
17	27	Remove Forms #2	1	8	9	10	11	2	2
19	21	Erect Forms #3	2	6	8	6	8	0	—*
21	23	Place Concrete #3	1	8	9	8	9	0	—*
23	25	Cure Concrete #3	1	9	10	9	10	0	—*
25	27	Remove Forms #3	1	10	11	10	11	0	—*

*Critical.

CHAPTER 6

6–1.

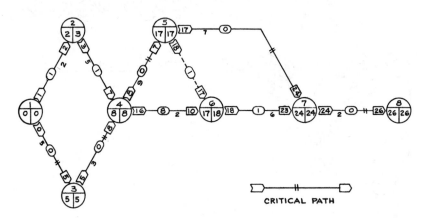

CRITICAL PATH

6-2.

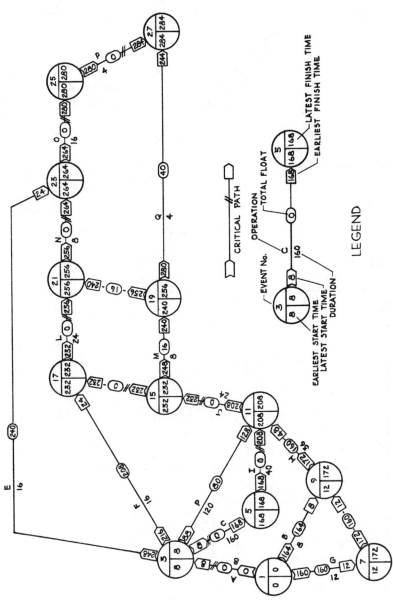

LEGEND

6–3.

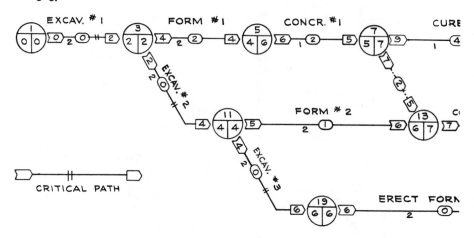

CRITICAL PATH

CHAPTER 7

7–1. *a)*

M	T	W	Th	F
OCT			19X3	
3	4	5	6	7
10	11	12	13	14
17	18	19	20	21
24 0	25 1	26 2	27 3	28 4
31 5				

M	T	W	Th	F
NOV			19X3	
	1 6	2 7	3 8	4 9
7 10	8 HOL	9 11	10 12	11 13
14 14	15 15	16 16	17 17	18 18
21 19	22 20	23 21	24 HOL	25 22
28 23	29 24	30 25		

DEC			19X3	
			1 26	2 27
5 28	6 29	7 30	8 31	9 32

b) Nov. 12 = day 14 (next working day).
c) 15 − 0 = 15 days.

6–3. (*Cont.*)

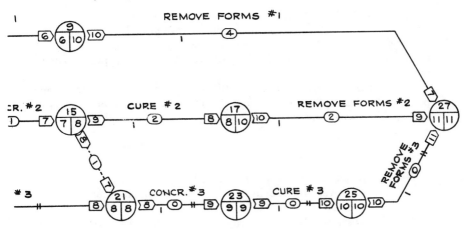

7–2.

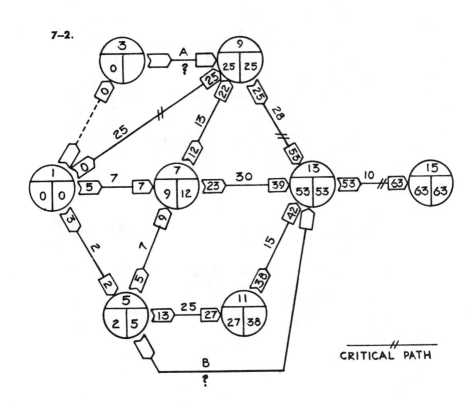

CRITICAL PATH

7–2. (*Cont.*)

For item A, the maximum time available is 25 days $(25 - 0 = 25)$. Hence, the proposal of Vendor Y should be chosen. The extra cost of Z's proposal is not justified, since it will not shorten the project time. On the other hand, X's proposal, while cheaper, would extend the project completion time.

For item B, 51 days are available $(53 - 2 = 51)$. Hence, the cheapest proposal (that of M) may be accepted. The delivery time of 45 days will not increase the project duration.

7–3. (Refer to solution of problem 5–2.)

    a) Improved valve delivery time is not advantageous since valve delivery is non-critical.

    b) There is no effect on project completion. The delay can be absorbed within the available float time.

    c) No effect on project completion; added time can be absorbed by available float time.

    d) Latest start of operation 1–9 (Deactivate) *minus* 8 hours:

$$164 - 8 = 156$$

    e) Time 244. (Earliest finish of 19–27: Reactivate.)

    f) The effect of the leak is to introduce two additional operations into the network between events 15 and 19. These are: Repair leak (16 hours) and Pressure test (8 hours). The earliest start of 21–23 becomes 264, and the entire project is delayed by 8 hours to a new completion time of 292.

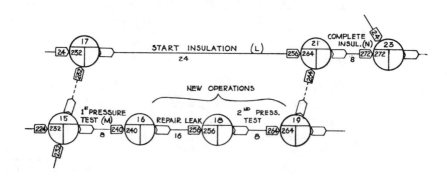

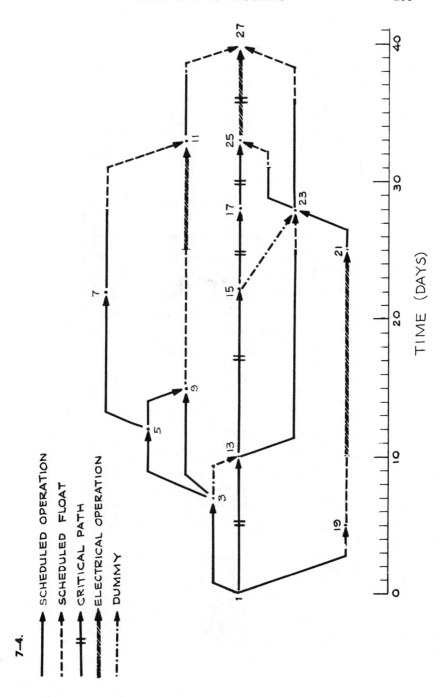

7-4.

→ SCHEDULED OPERATION

→ SCHEDULED FLOAT

→ CRITICAL PATH

→ ELECTRICAL OPERATION

→ DUMMY

TIME (DAYS)

See calculations on following page.

7-4. (Cont.)

| Node Numbers | | Descrip- tion | Duration | Earliest | | Latest | | Total Float | Scheduled | | Scheduled Float | Critical Operation | Electrical Operation |
i	j			Start	Finish	Start	Finish		Start	Finish			
1	3		7	0	7	3	10	3	0	7	—		
1	13		10	0	10	0	10	0	0	10	—	*	
1	19		5	0	5	7	12	7	0	5	5		
3	5		5	7	12	14	19	7	7	12	—		
3	9		8	7	15	19	27	12	7	15	10		
3	13		0	7	7	10	10	3	—	—	—		
5	7		10	12	22	19	29	7	12	22	—		
5	9		3	12	15	24	27	12	12	15	10		
7	11		6	22	28	29	35	7	22	28	5		#
9	11		8	15	23	27	35	12	25	33	—		
11	27		5	28	33	35	40	7	33	38	2		
13	15		12	10	22	10	22	0	10	22	—	*	
13	23		15	10	25	15	30	5	10	25	3		
15	17		6	22	28	22	28	0	22	28	—	*	
15	23		0	22	22	30	30	8	—	—	—		
17	23		5	28	33	28	33	0	28	33	—	*	
19	21		15	5	20	12	27	7	10	25	—		#
21	23		3	20	23	27	30	7	25	28	—		
23	25		3	25	28	30	33	5	28	31	2		
23	27		8	25	33	32	40	7	28	36	4		
25	27		7	33	40	33	40	0	33	40	—	*	#

CHAPTER 8

8–1.

Node Numbers				Earliest		Latest		Total Float
i	j	Description	Duration	Start	Finish	Start	Finish	
1	2	b	2	0	2	1	3	1
1	3	a	3	0	3	0	3	0*
1	7	c	2	0	2	5	7	5
2	3	Dummy	0	2	2	3	3	1
3	4	d	2	3	5	3	5	0*
4	5	g	1	5	6	7	8	2
4	8	e	1	5	6	7	8	2
4	6	f	1	5	6	5	6	0*
5	9	j	1	6	7	8	9	2
6	8	h	2	6	8	6	8	0*
7	8	k	1	2	3	7	8	5
8	9	i	1	8	9	8	9	0*

*Critical.

CPM Computations

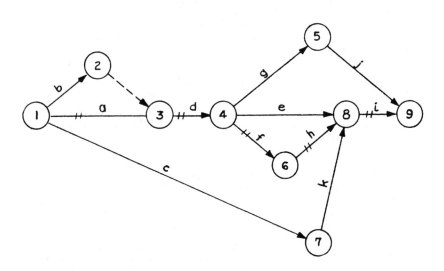

Critical Path

8–1. (*Cont.*)

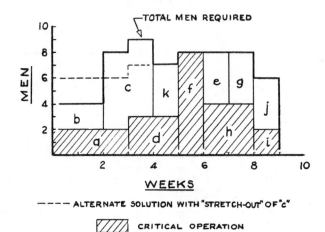

WEEKS

———— ALTERNATE SOLUTION WITH "STRETCH-OUT" OF "c"

▨▨▨ CRITICAL OPERATION

Manpower Schedule

8–2. *a*)

Operation	Men Required	Day Number														
		1	2	3	4	5	6	7	8	9	10	11	12	13	14	15
1-2	3	3	3	3												
1-3	2	2	2	2	2	2										
1-4	2				2	2										
2-5	1				1	1	1									
3-5	4						4	4	4	4						
4-6	1							1	1	1	1					
5-6	3										3	3	3			
Total		5	5	5	5	5	5	5	5	5	4	3	3			

b)

Operation	Men Required	Day Number														
		1	2	3	4	5	6	7	8	9	10	11	12	13	14	15
1-2	3	3	3	3												
1-3	2				2	2	2	2	2							
1-4	2				2	2										
2-5	1						1	1	1							
3-5	4									4	4	4	4			
4-6	1						1	1	1					1		
5-6	3													3	3	3
Total		3	3	3	4	4	4	4	4	4	4	4	4	4	3	3

8–2. *c*)

Operation	Man-Days	Day Number																		
		1	2	3	4	5	6	7	8	9	10	11	12	13	14	15	16	17	18	19
1-2	9	4	4	1																
1-3	10			3	4	3														
1-4	4						2	2												
2-5	3					1	2													
3-5	16							2	4	4	4	2								
4-6	4											2	2							
5-6	9												2	4	3					
Total		4	4	4	4	4	4	4	4	4	4	4	4	4	3					

CHAPTER 9

9–1. *a*) $2 \times 4 \times \$5 = \$40.$

    b) 4 hours.

    c) $3 \times 3 \times \$5 = \$45.$

    d) Crash duration = 3 hours.

    e)

$$\text{Cost slope} = \frac{\$45 - \$40}{4 - 3} = \$5 \text{ per hour}$$

9–2. *a*) Normal cost is $2,100; normal duration is 45 days.

    b) See Work Sheets No. 1, No. 2, and No. 3 on pages 238 and 239.

    c) A second critical path is introduced during the first shortening cycle.

    d) See graph on page 240.

    e)

SUMMARY OF DIRECT, INDIRECT, AND TOTAL COST

Duration (days)	Direct Cost ($)	Indirect Cost ($)	Total Cost ($)
45	2,100	1,700	3,800
42	2,220	1,550	3,770
39	2,340	1,400	3,740
34	2,640	1,150	3,790
32	2,880	1,050	3,930

Minimum total project cost is $3,740, at a duration of 39 days.

    f) The schedule for a 39-day duration is shown on Work Sheet No. 3 (page 239).

WORKSHEET NO. 1

Operation		Cost ($)		Duration (days)		Cost Increment (3)-(4)	Maximum Days Shortening (5)-(6)	Cost per Day To Shorten (7)÷(8) $/Day	Cycle						
i	j	Crash	Normal	Normal	Crash				0	1	2	3	4	5	6
(1)	(2)	(3)	(4)	(5)	(6)	(7)	(8)	(9)			Days Shortened				
1	2	720	600	20	17	120	3	40		3					
1	3	200	200	25	25	0	0	∞							
2	3	440	300	10	8	140	2	70					2		
2	4	700	400	12	6	300	6	50			3		2		
3	4	420	300	5	2	120	3	40				5			
4	5	600	300	10	5	300	5	60							
Total			$2,100												

	Cycle						
	0	1	2	3	4	5	6
a) Project Duration	45	42	39	34	32		
b) Total Number of Days Reduced	0	3	3	5	2		
c) Total Cost per Day To Shorten	-	40	40	60	120		
d) Increase in Cost	0	120	120	300	240		
e) New Project Cost	2,100	2,220	2,340	2,640	2,880		

WORKSHEET NO. 2

Operation		Critical Paths			Cost Slope $/Day	Cost To Shorten Cycle					
i	j					1	2	3	4		
1	2	⊗	⊗		40	40					
1	3			x	∞						
2	3	⊗			70				70		
2	4		x		50				50		
3	4	⊗		⊗	40		40				
4	5	⊗	⊗	⊗	60			60			
		Total				40	40	60	120		

WORKSHEET NO. 3

SCHEDULE SUMMARIES

Project Duration / Operation	Durations						
	45 (normal)	42	39*	34	32 (crash)		
1-2	20	17	17	17	17		
1-3	25	25	25	25	25		
2-3	10	10	10	10	8		
2-4	12	12	12	12	10		
3-4	5	5	2	2	2		
4-5	10	10	10	5	5		

*Optimum duration.

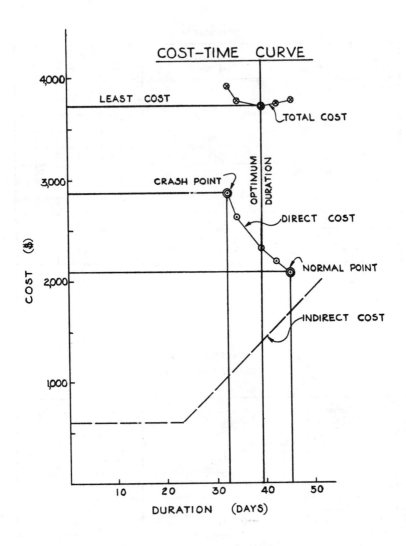

CHAPTER 10

10–1. *a)* $t_e = \dfrac{a + 4m + b}{6} = \dfrac{24 + 4(29) + 33}{6} \doteq \dfrac{173}{6} = 28.8.$

b) $\sigma = \dfrac{b - a}{6} = \dfrac{33 - 24}{6} = \dfrac{9}{6} = 1.5.$

c) $v = (\sigma)^2 = (1.5)^2 = 2.25.$

10–2. *Activity*   *Range* $(b - a)$
       1       $16 - 4 = 12$
       2       $40 - 33 = 7$
       3       $26 - 12 = 14$

Activity 3 has the greatest uncertainty.

10–3.

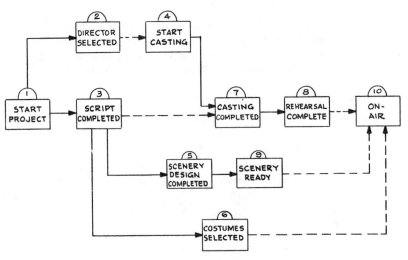

10–4. *a)* T_E (for event 5) $= 5 + 8 + 9 = 22.$

b)   *Operation*   *Variance* (v)
       1–2   4.0
       1–3   4.0
       2–5   9.0
       3–4   1.0
       4–5   2.25

10–4. *c*) V (for event 5) $= 4.0 + 1.0 + 2.25 = 7.25.$

     d) σ (for event 5) $= \sqrt{7.25} = 2.69.$

10–5. *a*) For $T_S = T_E$, probability $= 50$ per cent.

     b) $z = \dfrac{T_S - T_E}{\sigma_{T_E}} = \dfrac{28 - 30}{3} = \dfrac{-2}{3} = -0.667.$

From Table 10–1, probability $= 25$ per cent.

     c) $z = \dfrac{T_S - T_E}{\sigma_{T_E}} = \dfrac{35 - 30}{3} = \dfrac{+5}{3} = +1.67$

From Table 10–1, probability of completion $= 95$ per cent; hence, probability of *non*-completion $= 5$ per cent.

     d) $36 - 30 = 6 = 2\sigma$
         $\underline{30 - 24 = 6 = 2\sigma}$
                       4σ

The range of times represents a "spread" of 4 sigmas ($4 \times \sigma$). A spread of 4σ takes in 96 per cent of the total occurrences. Hence, 4 per cent of the roasts will require less than 24 minutes or more than 36 minutes. See page 153.

10–6. *a*)

Event Numbers		Times			Ex-pected Time	Critical Opera-tion	Stand-ard Devia-tion	Variance
		Opti-mistic	Most Likely	Pessi-mistic			$\sigma = \dfrac{b-a}{6}$	
i	*j*	*a*	*m*	*b*	t_e			$v = \sigma^2$
1	2	2	3	4	3	x	$\frac{2}{6} = \frac{1}{3}$	$\frac{1}{9}$
1	3	4	6	8	6	x	$\frac{4}{6} = \frac{2}{3}$	$\frac{4}{9}$*
1	4	4	5.5	10	6			
2	3	1	3	5	3	x	$\frac{4}{6} = \frac{2}{3}$	$\frac{4}{9}$
2	5	3	7.5	9	7			
3	4	6	7.5	12	8	x	$\frac{6}{6} = 1$	$1 = \frac{9}{9}$
3	6	3.5	5	6.5	5			
4	6	2	2.5	6	3	x	$\frac{4}{6} = \frac{2}{3}$	$\frac{4}{9}$
5	6	0.5	2	3.5	2			

* The variance along path 1–3 is $\frac{4}{9}$, which is less than the sum of variances along path 1–2–3, which is $\frac{5}{9}$. The largest sum is used.

10-6. *b*) and *c*)

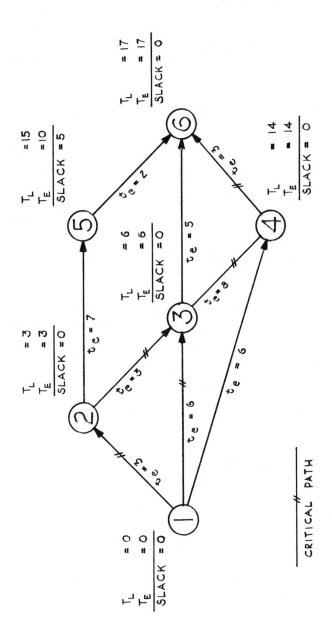

$T_L = 17$
$T_E = 17$
SLACK = 0

$T_L = 15$
$T_E = 10$
SLACK = 5

$t_e = 2$

$t_e = 3$

$T_L = 14$
$T_E = 14$
SLACK = 0

$T_L = 3$
$T_E = 3$
SLACK = 0

$t_e = 7$

$T_L = 6$
$T_E = 6$
SLACK = 0

$t_e = 5$

$t_e = 3$

$t_e = 8$

$t_e = 6$

$t_e = 6$

$t_e = 3$

$T_L = 0$
$T_E = 0$
SLACK = 0

CRITICAL PATH

10–6. *d*) For event 5, $T_S = T_E = 10$. Hence, there is a 50 per cent probability of reaching event 5 by this day.

e) Earliest completion time $= T_E$ for event 6 $= 17$.

f) and *g*) In summing variances, note that the critical path branches in going from event 1 to event 3. In this case we sum the variances over each branch and choose the larger sum, as follows:

Branch 1–2–3		*Branch 1–3*	
Operation	*Variance (v)*	*Operation*	*Variance (v)*
1–2	⅑	1–3	4⁄9
2–3	4⁄9		
Total	5⁄9		4⁄9

Sum of variances (*v*) to event 4:

$$V_4 = \frac{5}{9} + \frac{9}{9} = \frac{14}{9}$$

Probability of completing event 4 by day 13:

$$\sigma_4 = \sqrt{V_4} = \sqrt{\frac{14}{9}} = \sqrt{1.56} = 1.25$$

$$z = \frac{T_S - T_E}{\sigma_4} = \frac{13 - 14}{1.25} = \frac{-1}{1.25} = -0.8$$

From Table 10–1, for $z = -0.8$, probability $= 21$ per cent.

Sum of variances (*v*) to event 6:

$$V_6 = \frac{5}{9} + \frac{9}{9} + \frac{4}{9} = \frac{18}{9} = 2$$

Probability of completing event 6 by day 18:

$$\sigma_6 = \sqrt{V_6} = \sqrt{2} = 1.41$$

$$z = \frac{T_S - T_E}{\sigma_6} = \frac{18 - 17}{1.41} = \frac{+1}{1.41} = +0.71$$

From Table 10–1, for $z = +0.71$, probability of completion $= 76$ per cent. Thus, probability of non-completion $= 100 - 76 = 24$ per cent.

CHAPTER 11

11-1.

Node Numbers		Descrip- tion	Remaining Duration	Earliest		Latest		Float	
i	j			Start	Finish	Start	Finish	Total	Free
0	10		0	12	12	—	—	Completed	
0	20		1	12	13	36	37	24	0
0	30		0	12	12	14	14	Completed	
0	40		2	12	14	12	14	0	—*
10	70		—	—	32#	—	37	5	0
20	70		0	13	13	37	37	Completed	
30	50		10	14#	24	14	24	0	—*
30	60		15	12#	27	22	37	10	0
30	70		5	12·	17	32	37	20	15
40	50		10	14	24	14	24	0	—*
50	70		0	24	24	37	37	13	8
50	80		8	24	32	24	32	0	—*
60	90		10	27	37	37	47	10	10
70	90		10	32	42	37	47	5	5
80	90		15	32	47	32	47	0	—*

*Critical operation.
#Scheduled date.

11-2.

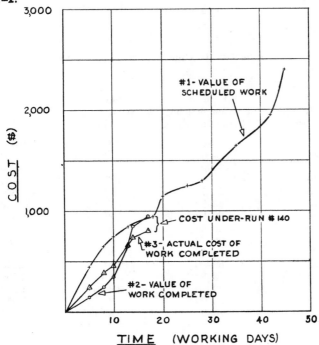

11–2. (*Cont.*)

CPM COMPUTATIONS

Node Numbers				Earliest		Latest		Total
i	j	Description	Dura-tion	Start	Finish	Start	Finish	Float
0	10		10	0	10	0	10	0*
0	20		5	0	5	22	27	22
0	30		5	0	5	2	7	2
0	40		8	0	8	4	12	4
10	70		25	10	35	10	35	0*
20	70		8	5	13	27	35	22
30	50		15	5	20	7	22	2
30	60		15	5	20	25	40	20
30	70		15	5	20	20	35	15
40	50		10	8	18	12	22	4
50	70	Dummy	0	20	20	35	35	15
50	80		8	20	28	22	30	2
60	90		5	20	25	40	45	20
70	90		10	35	45	35	45	0*
80	90		15	28	43	30	45	2

*Critical.

a)

Curve No. 1: Value of Scheduled Work

Day Number	Operation Scheduled for Completion (early finish)	Value (estimated cost) ($)	Cumulative Value ($)
5	0–20	300	–
5	0–30	150	450
8	0–40	200	650
10	0–10	100	750
13	20–70	100	850
18	40–50	100	950
20	30–50	100	–
20	30–60	40	–
20	30–70	60	1,150
20	50–70	Dummy	–
25	60–90	100	1,250
28	50–80	50	1,300
35	10–70	350	1,650
43	80–90	300	1,950
45	70–90	450	2,400

11–2. *b*)

Curve No. 2: Value of Work Completed

Day Number	Operation Completed	Estimated Cost ($)	Cumulative Value ($)
5	0–30	150	150
8	20–70	100	250
10	0–10	100	350
13	0–20	300	650
14	0–40	200	850
17	30–50	100	950

As of day 17, value of work completed ($950) exceeds value of scheduled work (approximately $930). Hence, project is ahead of schedule.

c)

Curve No. 3: Cost of Work Completed

Day Number	Operation Completed	Actual Cost ($)	Cumulative Value ($)
5	0–30	250	250
8	20–70	130	380
10	0–10	90	470
13	0–20	190	680
14	0–40	70	830
17	30–50	80	910

Cost underrun = $950 − $910 = $40.

CHAPTER 14

14–1. The following contract clause is intended to be suggestive, rather than a definite answer to the problem:

PROGRESS CONTROL AND REPORTING

a) Upon award of contract, each Subcontractor shall cooperate with the General Contractor to develop a detailed construction schedule, herein called the FINAL SCHEDULE, using Critical Path Method techniques. For this purpose, he shall make available key supervisory personnel familiar with the Work. It is anticipated that preparation of the FINAL SCHEDULE will require approximately _____ weeks.

b) The FINAL SCHEDULE will show each operation required for the work, the sequence in which the operations must be performed, the number of days required for each operation, and the contractor or other agency responsible for accomplishment. When approved, the FINAL SCHEDULE shall become a part of the Contract.

c) Each Subcontractor shall report the progress of his work under the Contract bi-weekly, according to a schedule and in a format to be prescribed by the General Contractor. The report shall include the following information:

(1) For each operation completed during the reporting period, date completed

(2) For each operation in progress but not yet completed, the number of days' work remaining to complete

(3) Operations, if any, that the Subcontractor feels were omitted from the chart and should be added

(4) Operations the Subcontractor feels are no longer required and should be dropped

(5) Proposed changes in the sequence of operations

(6) Anticipated or proposed changes in time estimates of operations not yet started

(7) A list of "hold-up items" that shall include items requiring expediting by the Owner, consultant, or any contractor, which may delay or are delaying the work

d) Each Subcontractor shall make every effort to commence and complete each operation as early as possible, and in no case later than the time called for on the FINAL SCHEDULE.

e) In the event of an actual or anticipated delay in the progress of his work, the Subcontractor shall promptly notify the General Contractor, and if the delay is not caused by others, shall take corrective action to overcome or prevent it. Such action may include, but is not limited to, any of the following:

> Use of additional manpower
> Working overtime
> Use of multiple shifts
> Payments of bonuses to sub-subcontractors
> or material suppliers
> Changing sequence of operations

f) If the delay is due to causes within the control of the Subcontractor, then the added cost, if any, of corrective action shall be borne by the responsible Subcontractor.

g) Should the Subcontractor fail to take effective corrective action, or to comply with the General Contractor's directive for preventing or overcoming the delay, and further, should a delay actually occur, then the General Contractor may direct that the lost time be made up by working overtime by the Subcontractor or any other Subcontractor, or by other means. In such a case, the added cost, if any, shall be back-charged against the Subcontractor causing the delay.

h) Whether or not a delay shall be caused by or be the responsibility of a Subcontractor, such Subcontractor shall, upon written order of the General Contractor so to do, take all such corrective action and other measures as may be necessary or appropriate to prevent or overcome such delay and as may be specified by the General Contractor in such order.

i) If the delay is not the responsibility of the Subcontractor, then the General Contractor, at his option, may order overtime or other corrective action at the General Contractor's expense or may grant an extension of completion time.

j) An extension of completion time shall be the Subcontractor's sole remedy for any delay, except where the General Contractor has authorized corrective action at his expense, in which case this shall constitute the Subcontractor's sole remedy for such delay, and the Subcontractor shall not be entitled to an extension of completion time or to any other remedy.

k) No extension for delay, regardless of the cause therefor, shall be granted, unless the Subcontractor shall have notified the General Contractor in writing within seven (7) days after the occurrence of the delay. A request for extension of time shall specify the operation or operations affected, the cause of the delay, and the amount of time requested. In the case of a continuing cause of delay, only one claim is necessary.

l) A delay may be considered as not being the Subcontractor's responsibility only where it is caused by act or neglect of the General Contractor, another Subcontractor, Owner or his employees, or by a separate contractor employed by the Owner, or by changes in the Work, or by labor disputes, fire, unusual delay in transportation, unavoidable casualties, or by other cause which the Architect, acting under the terms of the contract between General Contractor and Owner, may determine is beyond the General Contractor's control.

m) Where the General Contractor directs overtime work, multiple shift work or other expediting action by a Subcontractor for any reason other than to make up a delay or lost time caused by the same Subcontractor, then the added cost, if any, shall be considered "extra work," and the contract price shall be adjusted accordingly.

Index